W9-BGP-924

Beginner's
HUNGARIAN

Beginner's
HUNGARIAN

Katalin Boros
of Eurolingua

HIPPOCRENE BOOKS
New York

Copyright© 1994 by Eurolingua.

All rights reserved.

For information, address:
HIPPOCRENE BOOKS, INC.
171 Madison Avenue
New York, NY 10016

ISBN 0-7818-0209-1

Printed in the United States of America.

TABLE OF CONTENTS

INTRODUCTION

The rich culture and languages of Eastern Europe are unique, intricate and subtle, steeped in tradition by hundreds of years of history. But, since the Eastern European countries were closed societies for over 40 years under communist rule, little is known about them.

After the fall of the Iron Curtain a flurry of activity is being spurred throughout Eastern Europe by the desire to establish democratic institutions and free market economies. Firms from the West are exploring business opportunities and expansion into these virtually untapped markets. A fresh and beautiful land together with the rich and exciting cultural heritage of its people has opened up for tourists to explore.

As a result, EUROLINGUA was started in September, 1990 to meet the growing demand for Eastern European languages and cross-cultural instructions. EUROLINGUA primarily serves tourists and business people who deal in international trade.

The passionate traveler would like to understand and enjoy the people and the customs of the country he will visit. For a successful international transaction the businessman has to know the appropriate conduct in various business situations. Finally, basic information about geography, history and politics of the country to be visited, together with some language knowledge will make anyone feel more at home.

These considerations have brought about this book, in the hope that it will become your friend and guide during your trip. The knowledge of customs, manners and some basics of language will help you discover more exiting things and make more friends than you have ever dreamed.

The book has two parts. The first part gives you information about the country (geography, history, economy, culture, customs and manners) and the second part consists of language lessons.

The language lessons are designed for the traveler and the non-specialist amateur. You will learn useful phrases and words for special situations and basic grammar hints. The lessons will not cover all grammatical problems, nor will they give a rich vocabulary for sophisticated conversation. Instead they will teach you enough to feel comfortable in a variety of situations, which you will find described here.

With this small, compact book you will have in your pocket a collection of bits of information, sufficient to carry out satisfying interaction with the people of the country you visit, in their own language. It is the result of many hours of work, research and travel done by enthusiastic teachers and travelers who wish you good luck in your study and a wonderful trip.

GEOGRAPHY

Hungary is situated in Central Europe, occupying an area of 93,032 square kilometers (35,910 square miles). It is encircled by the Alps, the Carpathians and the Dinaric Alps. Hungary is an inland country that borders Austria, Slovakia, Ukraine, Romania, Yugoslavia and Croatia.

Almost two-thirds of the country's territory consists of fertile plains, no more than 200 meters (656 feet) above the sea level. The highest peak is Kékestető, 1,015 meters (3,330 feet) in the Mátra Mountains. The lowest point is 78 meters (256 feet) which is near Szeged.

Hungary is divided into three large regions: Transdanubia (Dunántúl), the Great Plains (Alföld) and Northern Hungary.

The longest river in the country is the Tisza, 579 kilometers. The best known is the Danube. Its Hungarian portion is 417 kilometers long.

Spreading over an area of 596 square kilometers (230 square miles), Lake Balaton is the largest lake of Central and Western Europe. In the summer the water temperature is usually above 22°C (72°F). In the winter the surface of the lake frequently freezes. Lake Velence, the country's second largest lake lies between Budapest and the Balaton.

Hungary is rich in mineral waters. There are about 80 thermal springs in Budapest alone.

Hungary's climate belongs into the temperate zone. Temperatures above 30°C (90°F) may occur in July and August but generally do not last very long. January is the coldest month, but the average temperature does not fall below -1°C (30°F).

The flora and fauna offer a great deal of variety. There are 2,165 flowering plants and 32,000 different kinds of animals living on the territory of the country.

Hungary has a high density of population with an average of 114 inhabitants per square kilometer. The total number of the population is 10,590,000. The population of the capital is 2,115,000. There are eight cities besides Budapest with a population of over 100,000: Miskolc, Debrecen, Szeged, Pécs, Győr, Nyíregyháza, Kecskemét and Székesfehérvár.

Budapest, the capital of Hungary is situated on the two banks of the Danube. The hillsides of Buda is to the west and to the east is the flat expanse of Pest. The two banks are connected by eight bridges. Budapest is the center of the political, economical and cultural life of Hungary.

HISTORY AND POLITICS

Where Hungarians originate from is still a question much debated by historians, ethnographers and anthropologists. Most would agree that Hungarian tribes had journeyed from the northern slopes of the Ural Mountains toward the Carpathian basin, arriving there around 895 AD. The seven nomadic tribes found fertile fields, good grazing grounds and ancient tribal societies. Although it took some time for them to get used to a permanent homeland (adventurous Hungarians made "excursions" to as far as the Iberian peninsula). The first king, St. Stephen (997 - 1038), succeeded in introducing his subjects to Christianity and to a more stable lifestyle.

Although the Kingdom of Hungary weathered the Tartars (early 13th century) and other invaders, it was a major European power until 1526 when it fell to the Ottoman Empire. The Turks ruled much of Hungary for a century-and-a-half. In 1686, Hungarians succeeded in throwing off the Turkish yoke, only to come under the rule of the Austrian Habsburgs. Several ill-fated wars of independence attempted to free Hungary unsuccessfully. The two most notable ones were led by Ferenc Rákóczi from 1706 to 1711, and Lajos Kossuth from 1848 to 1849. In 1867, the weakening Habsburg Empire struck a deal with the antagonistic Hungarians and established the dual Austro-Hungarian monarchy that afforded similar rights to the two most important components of this multi-ethnic entity.

Ethnic strife in the monarchy was ultimately the pretext for the outbreak of World War I which resulted not only in the breakup of the Empire, but also Hungary's loss of one half of its territory and a third of its population. The Treaty of Trianon (1920), that meted out such a harsh judgment on the country, is still a symbol of national tragedy to Hungarians. During the inter-war period Hungary enjoyed economic growth but increasing economic disparity among the social classes. The authoritarian regime of Admiral Horty hedged its bets on the Germans' side and was unable to prevent the country from active participation in World War II.

Hungary was liberated from the German occupying forces by the Soviet Army in 1945. Following a period of multiparty system, the Soviets and their Hungarian followers took their gloves off in 1948 and established a totalitarian Communist dictatorship. In the fall of 1956 a popular revolution occurred that was bloodily repressed by Soviet forces. After 1956, however, the slow and very gradual process of political and economic liberalization began. Although the country's democratic changes should not be overestimated, Hungary became the "merriest barrack" in the Communist Bloc. Hungary's post-Communist democratization began in 1988. A multi-party system was approved by the ruling Communists and in 1990 democratic elections were held after four decades. The elections were won by the center-right Hungarian Democratic Forum that formed a coalition government with the Christian Democratic People's Party and the Independent Smallholders' Party in May. The most important opposition parties are the Federation of Free Democrats, the Federation of Young Democrats, and the Hungarian Socialist Party.

4

The new government faces the difficult task of taking the political democratization process to its conclusion and to rescue Hungary from its current economic predicament. In June 1991, the last soldiers of the occupying Soviet Army left Hungary. Budapest is also intent on leaving the Warsaw Pact and gaining membership in the European Community. Economic restructuring has begun, including the denationalization of some industries and the reorganization of the banking system. Although the government has had to deal with several domestic political crises, it seems to be beyond question that the country is well on the way of becoming a stable multiparty democracy.

DOING BUSINESS IN HUNGARY[1]

Long before its transition to democracy in the year of 1989, Hungary has enacted market based corporate and foreign investment policies with the intention to attract foreign investment. Although at this time Hungarian companies still labored under a centrally planned economic regime, these economic reforms[2] provided the ground work for the new changes at the dawn of political thawing, signaled most visibly by the fall of the Berlin Wall. This was the time when this quasi-free market system, the so-called "goulash communism", responded to the new political order in Europe with insatiable hunger to become a part of the economic house of the west. She set out to achieve this task, among other things, by enacting new laws to encourage foreign economic involvement in Hungary.

Hungary's appeal to foreign investors, aside from its legal infrastructure, lies in several factors, each having its special importance: (a) its relatively low cost labor force; (b) highly skilled work force, especially in technical fields; (c) proximity and access to Western European markets, and its decades long experience in convertible currency dealings; and (d) the sometimes discounted asset of its proximity, and well developed nexus to the markets of the Soviet Union, or its legal successor.

Three pieces of legislation provide the basic framework for the encouragement of foreign capital flow into Hungary. The first such body of law is the 1988 Foreign Investment Act (as amended in 1991) which provides the legal framework for foreign investment. This article enables a foreign investor to establish a legal entity in Hungary with or without Hungarian participation, or as an alternative, to participate in an ongoing Hungarian operation in the form of a joint venture, or otherwise. Furthermore, this legislation provides the foreign investor with certain tax benefits in some circumstances, as well as it greatly reduces the bureaucratic requirements for the registration of a foreign company, or joint venture.

The second such body of law is the 1988 Company Act VI., which provides for the various legal forms Hungarian private enterprises may take under Hungarian law. This law also provides foreign entities, operating in Hungary, with the same treatment as Hungarian state and private companies would enjoy.

This article is based upon laws in force on March 8, 1991, and does not purport to represent any laws subsequently enacted in Hungary.

The 1968 New Economic Mechanism attempted to introduce market incentives and decentralization into Hungary's centrally planned economy in a unique way. While the state abstained from making central plans, the individual company managers, whom were elected by the companies' workers, negotiated their production quotas, prices, etc., directly with the state. This proved to be an incentive based system, for if a company was successful in its endeavors, its managers received bonuses.

Finally, the last piece of legislation pertinent in this section is the Act XIII. 1989 on the Transformation of Business Organizations and Companies. This Act permits the privatization of state enterprises, and envisions foreign ownership of the thus privatized companies. This is an especially noteworthy Act, for Hungary could privatize U.S.$ 32 billion worth of state assets and is planning to privatize 32 billion dollars worth of assets by the end of 1991.

Concerning export - import activities with Hungarian companies one should be aware, that in case of imports into Hungary, the Hungarian currency is **de facto** convertible for those products which are considered liberalized. In other words, the Hungarian company acquiring the liberalized products, may exchange its Hungarian currency, the Forint, at a local bank in order to fulfill its payment obligations to its western exporter. However, for the imports of products not being considered liberalized, the foreign currency exchange controls and procedures remain to be strict. Therefore, the exporter is well advised to verify whether its product is on the liberalized list or not. The range of liberalized products is rapidly growing, and by now represents perhaps more than 90% of all products.

Hungary is the member of various international trade organizations, such as the International Monetary Fund, the International Bank for Reconstruction and Development, the International Finance Corporation, the General Agreement of Trade Tariffs, the Overseas Private Insurance Corporation and the World Intellectual Property Organization. For specific projects, and upon proper showing of a sound business plan, some of the above mentioned organizations provide credit and/or equity financing or investment insurance.

Accounting in Hungary is done by Hungarian statutory rules, which historically had little resemblance to the well established accounting principles of the Western World. Recently, however, Hungary appeared to move closer to the European Economic Community (EEC), by its new Act on Accounting, which is based on the accounting system of the EEC. This new accounting system was due to be introduced beginning January 1, 1991.

ARTS IN HUNGARY

There is a Hungarian proverb which says that "a nation lives by and through its language". Hungary is a small country. Its language is practically inaccessible to the outside world. So we must feel grateful to **music**, this international language which knows no boundaries.

At the end of the 9th century, the "magyar" tribes, originating from Central Asia, settled in the Carpathian basin which became, and is today, Hungary. Adopting Christianity under its first king, St. Stephen, in the 11th century, cultural life followed the pattern found elsewhere in the medieval kingdoms of Western Europe with whom contact was maintained. Thus, musical life was dual. To serve the Church by religious songs and gregorian chants and also to entertain the laity with folksongs, historic lore and ballads performed by wandering minstrels in the countryside. Such cultural and musical activities certainly reached their zenith in the splendid 15th century renaissance court of King Matthias in Buda.

In the 16th century, Hungary fell and remained under Turkish occupation for 150 years. Impoverished, savaged and cut off from the West, it could not partake in the stupendous transformation of musical history during the Renaissance when music emerged as an autonomous art.

From the beginning of the 18th century until the end of World War I., Hungary was dominated by and formed part of the Habsburg empire. While the overwhelming cultural influence was German, the numerous uprisings against Austrian oppression gave birth to soldiers' songs with typical Hungarian flavor (verbunkos). During the 18th century, Hungary certainly cannot rival the giants of the German and Italian baroque, except perhaps to claim that Bach was of Hungarian origin. However, on the large aristocratic estates the cultivation of music was on par with the Viennese model. Joseph Haydn spent a large part of his life at the estate of the Eszterházy Princes. His acquaintance with Hungarian musical idioms is reflected in many of his compositions.

The significant intensification of the 19th century musical life in Hungary was mainly centered in the capital, Budapest. Composers, like Ferenc Erkel, composed noteworthy operas; concerts by visiting artists multiplied, (Beethoven himself visited Hungary); but what the world recognized as Hungarian music was produced by the famous and ever present gipsy bands. Their many songs and dances (i.e., csárdás), were, in a large part, not original folklore. Written in a pleasant "folksy" idiom, sentimental or fiery, they constituted the main fare of musical entertainment, and as great composers as Ferenc Liszt and Brahms adapted this style into their numerous Hungarian flavored compositions. But it was only at the outset of the 20th century that the folklore research of two of the greatest composers, Béla Bartók and Zoltán Kodály, discovered the whole treasure-house (in outlying villages and armed with primitive phonographs) of thousands of original and very ancient songs. They were discussed, analyzed, catalogued and edited, and as a stunning surprise, it was found that many of those songs were in the pentatonic - five note - scale, which musicologists definitely consider as Asiatic in origin. Thus, the memory of those archetypal pagan songs must have survived orally for thousands of years!

On the western musical scene Hungary only emerged as a "superpower" in the latter part of the 19th century. Joseph Joachim, one of the most celebrated violinists of the period, friend of Mendelssohn and Brahms, was Hungarian. His pupil, Jenő Hubay in Budapest, Leopold Auer in St. Petersburg, Carl Flesh in Berlin - all of them Hungarians - were the most sought after violin pedagogues of their era. Ernő Dohnányi, a great pianist and a significant composer himself, taught generations of Hungarian pianists who achieved world wide reputation. They were followed in our time by Leó Reiner, György Széll, Jenő Ormandy and George Solti, and also by great string quartets such as the Waldbauer quartet, (five of Bartók's quartets were dedicated to them), the Lener, the original Budapest, the Roth and the Hungarian quartets, who were all household names on five continents. This trend is continuing.

Yet, perhaps all of the above is overshadowed in significance by Béla Bartók's and Zoltán Kodály's emergence. Bartók is universally recognized as one of the greatest - if not the greatest - composers of our century. Kodály, besides having been an important composer, was the founder of a widely acclaimed teaching method of musical education (bearing his name) and also the teacher of a whole string of young composers who achieved fame like two of the most recognized figures in today's avant-garde, György Ligeti and György Kurtágh.

It is a sad fact, that most of the medieval **architecture** and sculptures of the basilicas and monastic churches, ravaged by wars, the mongolian invasion and 150 years of Turkish occupation left us with only broken fragments scattered in the uncovered sites of the Hungarian plains. The Benedictine roman-gothic church of **Ják**, preserving its sculpture-ornamented facade and its interior space divisions, is a rare survivor.

The non-occupied territories in the north (now Slovakia) and Transylvania to the east (now incorporated into Romania), settled by people fleeing from the center, fared better. One of our most valued relics, the bronze horseback statue of St. George terracing the dragon from the metal shop of the Kolozsvári brothers still stands in Prague, while other bronzes known to have come from their hands were melted down for Turkish cannons.

Preserved in those off-beat areas and now collected in the Budapest National Gallery and the Esztergom Christian Museum, are the many polyptychs, beautiful winged altar pieces with some exquisite wood carved figures surrounded by panel paintings of legendary and biblical scenes. The so-called M.S. master's panels of the visitation and crucifixion, certainly rank with the great creations of International Gothic.

Due to the extensive archeological excavations undertaken after the severe destruction of the Castle area in World War II., many of our buried treasures came to light. Fragments from the 13th century palace of King Sigismund in Buda with some beautifully preserved and most expressive gothic heads, some of them displaying definitely individual "native" features.

While Chronicles had many reports about the early influx of the Italian Renaissance art to the Hungarian royal court, the excavations now also make it possible to reconstruct at least in one's imagination, the splendor of King Matthias's renaissance palace at the very same site. Ceilings decorated by a profusion of frescoes, halls and door frames covered by marble reliefs in red marble, a native material mined from the quarries near Esztergom. Chronicles at the Court tell about cart-loads of the material arriving day after day. On some days more than 60 of them! A visit to these excavations, which are still under way, and the reconstruction is certainly not a thing to be missed. Of course, everybody knows about Matthias's world famous library, though only 170 of his illustrated codexes (Corvina) have survived and only 40 of them are in Hungary. His court was also a very important humanistic center with figures such as Janus Pannonius, a leader in the movement to re-establish classical studies.

Hungarian architecture, sculpture or painting cannot measure up to the masterworks of the baroque period. The counter-reformation churches, the palaces of the aristocracy were built by "imported" artists, while many "native" artists had to leave the country in search for a living.

It was only during the 19th century that a movement for the renewal of Hungarian art began to gain force, propagated by writers and the sculptor István Ferenczy. While his inspiration was second-hand classicism from Rome, his young and talented follower, Miklós Izsó represents a break-through. A romantic, original artist, he chose ordinary, local people for his theme, as in his excellent marble statue of the "Lovelorn Shepherd", and in his terra-cottas of drinking, dancing villagers and gypsies.

Architecture also underwent an initially neo-classical revival. In the work of Joseph Hild, the architect of the Esztergom Basilica (with P. Kuhnel) the Eger Cathedral and many public and private buildings in the growing and expanding Pest side of the capital. Certainly the most important, purely classicistic building in the city is Pollock's National Museum, also dating from this period.

In architecture too, there was a turn toward romanticism. The most successful expression of the trend is represented by Frigyes Feszl's Vigadó Concert Hall. This was followed by the later eclecticist Miklós Ybl's neo-renaissance Opera House (with its interior ceiling decoration by the charming though rather lightweight frescoes of K. Lotz) Imre Steindl's neo-gothic Parliament, Frank Schulek's rebuilt Coronation Church (Matthias Church) and his decorative Fishermen's Bastion of romanesque inspiration.

Then trying to "secede" from the established styles of the past and create a new Hungarian architecture, we might mention Ödön Lechner's buildings, (i.e., the Museum of Applied Arts, the Postal Savings Bank).

As in the other arts, the picture is rather bleak until the 19th century with respect to **painting**. The country was impoverished and the court of attraction for those able to afford its offerings, was Vienna. Károly Markó, a most accomplished landscape painter did most of his work in Rome and Florence. He gained fame with his compositions recalling the atmosphere of Claude Lorrain's.

After the failure of the 1848-49 revolution and the ensuing Austrian rule of terror, the works of Viktor Madarász, while in the prevalent academic tradition of the period, give expression to his despair, by depicting the fate of rebels and martyrs of the past, perhaps most tellingly by the "Mourning of László Hunyadi", the victim of royal treason.

The change in the mood of the country after the 1867 concordat is then represented in the academic-historic paintings of Gyula Benczur, a lover of lavish colors, rich textures, glamorously elaborated environments, perhaps best exemplified in his almost Roubensian "Baptism of Vajk". He was a technically accomplished painter, as was his contemporary, Bertalan Székely.

However, the genius of Mihály Munkácsy surpassed them all. He spent most of his life in Paris, but his paintings reflect the observations of his poor Hungarian village background and his unique temperament. He painted night prowlers, outcasts, foragers in a forest, landscapes too. Already as a young man, he became world famous with his "Prisoner on death row" painting. His colors are dark, even more darkened by time, with dramatic bursts of color, or white. Of great emotional intensity, focused on the tensions within the painting and evoking them in the spectator.

His friend, László Paál, attached himself to the Barbizon school and became an outstanding representative of that group with his "intimate landscapes".

Pál Szinyei-Merse independently experimented with and used the pure colors introduced by the impressionists and was met with equal derision at first, but is recognized by now as probably our best plein-air painter.

Between the two wars and again after the sixties, many individual artists came to the fore and artists' colonies multiplied in various parts of the country. The works by all of the artists mentioned, as well as of those left out by necessity, can be seen at the comprehensive collection of the National Gallery of Buda, and many works by the newest generation are exhibited in public parks and places and in galleries both in the capital and in other cities.

Hungarians are a singing nation, but due to the language barriers, the unique sound pattern and many grammatical features of the language, their **poetry** remained barely accessible to the West.

Yet, vernacular songs abound already from early times and throughout the nation's history. Religious and patriotic ones, celebratory or mournful about the state of the country, love songs and flower songs, others in the troubadour tradition of chivalry, or songs on the hard lot and courage fighting at the frontiers against treacherous Turks, or renegades to the Austrian cause. Some names stand out (Bálint Balassi, Mihály Csokonai, Dániel Berzsenyi) but a treasure house of expressive and memorable anonymous folksongs, ballads, legends, histories (chansons de geste) were transmitted orally and collected only later.

The true flowering of Hungarian **literature**, however, had to wait until the 19th century. Again, poetry led the way when Mihály Vörösmarty (1800 - 1855) burst onto the scene with his national epic - in resounding hexameters - on the conquest of the country to become Hungary by Árpád, chieftain of the seven magyar tribes at the end of the 9th century. A romantic poet, an ardent patriot, follower of Kossuth, he was crushed by the defeat of the revolution. One of his last poems, "The Old Gipsy", a somber and fiery meditation on the state of a strife-torn Earth, but ending on a note of hope for a better world to come. This is one of the greatest masterpieces of Hungarian poetry.

His younger compatriot, Sándor Petőfi (1823 - 1849) achieved world renown and has been translated into 50 different languages. The directness of his appeal, whether lyrical or revolutionary, is of an unmatched immediacy. Every perception of nature, of whatever everyday situation and expressed in the simplest of terms, becomes magically transposed into poetry. A radical, flamboyant personality. His "Song of the Nation" (Rise up Hungarians), delivered from the steps of the National Museum at the onset of the 1848 Revolution, electrified the entire country. His love poem, "At the end of September", written to his young wife, is one of the great love poems of all ages. Sadly prophetic too, it predicts his death as an unknown soldier at the battlefield near Segesvár and her marriage not long after his disappearance there.

His friend and peer, János Arany (1817 - 1882) is an entirely different personality. Retiring, gentle, with a fine sense of humor, extremely well read and a painstaking artist, he yet never lost touch with people. He is certainly our greatest narrative poet. His Toldi Trilogy takes up a rudimentary 16th century verse chronicle about a 14th century folktale and turns it into a practically modern psychological "novel". His virtuosity in using every resource of the language also shows in his translations, and aren't Hungarians lucky to have Hamlet and Midsummer night's dream translated by such a great artist!

Certainly the most popular novelist of the period was Mór Jókay, an excellent and prolific author of more than 100 novels of quasi historical but mostly imaginative fiction. Many of his books are still widely read and have been translated into several different languages.

At the beginning of the 20th century, Hungarian writers, poets, essayists established the literary magazine **"Nyugat"**. The name itself "West" stands for its motto and attracts most of the avant-garde artists. Foremost among them, Endre Ady. He visited Paris, was familiar with the poetry of Baudelaire, Rimbaud, Verlaine and he was open to their iconoclastic rage. He revolutionized and renewed Hungarian poetry.

His equally great follower, Attila József was the voice of the underprivileged proletariate and excelled in the ruthlessly realistic presentation of their deprivations and poverty.

Other **Nyugat** authors included the populist Zsigmond Móritz who portrayed in his novels the agricultural under-class and peasant life in appropriately juicy language. While Dezső Kosztolányi was an urban and urbane poet in love with the city and the people milling on its street, often raising in his poems the everyday hopes and frustrations of the average city dweller to universal questions about life and death. Mihály Babits, the editor of **Nyugat** for many years, embraced all the new trends and was a leading figure among the literati, firmly grounded in world literature. He was also a distinguished translator. His translation of the Divine Comedy is considered as a supreme achievement in any language.

Today's Hungarian writers, as do those of most countries around the globe, speak through many voices. Sometimes, though not often enough, their words are also heard beyond their frontiers.

Certainly a word has to be said about the popular **arts and crafts** of the Hungarian people, from the ornamentation of everyday utensils to the fineries of feast and ritual. Such decorative interests were obviously shared by all ethnic groups since time immemorial, but certainly lost ground during the industrial age, although we might hope for their revival in our more ethno-conscious time.

The oldest, and by now rare creations of village artists have become treasures of museums (e.g., the Ethnographic Museum in Budapest) and collectors' items.

So what are we talking about? In fact, if many of the symbolic connotations of crafting have disappeared, at the same time many aspects of those traditions survive.

The glazed tiles with figures or geometric decoration used for the surfacing of the tall, wood-burning hearths that heated the halls of the wealthy and also the so-called "beautiful room" of the village hamlet, providing excellent insulation and slow heat, go back to the 13th century, but were still produced and in use in our lifetime.

Wardrobes are latecomers on the village scene. Brides-to-be assembled their dowry, hand embroided bedcover and pillows, the Sunday attire of fine needlework and lace and often elaborate embroidery of a skirt, vest, blouse and apron, and of course, the wedding dress (often passed on from generation to generation) in marriage coffers, (cassoni) always painted, usually with floral motives, most frequently with tulips. Actually, they were called "tulip chests". At wedding time, these coffers were carried by the grooms' best men to their new home.

Many of the Hungarian villagers still produce these traditional embroideries (i.e., Kalocsa, Mezőkövesd), the motives, colors, stitch-work differing from one place to the other, but then much of it is done for the tourist trade or export (Hungarian blouses) and it takes a connoisseur's eye to separate the grain from the chaff.

The woodwork of cabinetmakers, the sculptured and often painted chairs, bedsteads, the carved and painted fences and porches, the ironwork of village smiths, and last but not least the output of village potters, again, using different designs according to the handed down traditions of the area, were also often raised to the level of **art** by the genius of talented individuals.

We must also mention the unique creations of our 20th century village pottery artist, Margit Kovács, whose works can be admired in her gallery at the delightful arts and crafts town of Szentendre which is only some 12 miles from Budapest.

PRACTICAL ADVICE FOR EVERYDAY LIFE

1. LOCATION

When asking for directions, the answer you will receive will not be
based upon point of compass or distance estimation by city blocks.
Usually, the starting point will be a well known area (i.e., a
certain street, square, theater, department store, etc.), and your
directions will say whether to turn left or right or to go straight
ahead (not by north, east, south or west parameters). Also, the
distance will be given in meters instead of feet, if the location
one seeks is near by. Longer distances will be expressed in
kilometers. One meter equals 3.3 feet and one kilometer equals .6
miles.

2. GROUND TRANSPORTATION

a. Mass transportation

The most common way to reach your destination in Hungary is by the
great network of public transportation. Every city has adequate
bus routes and a few larger cities have buses and trams (rapid
rail). You can also find underground and trolley cars in the
capital to accommodate the large volume of passenger flow. If you
choose to ride on a bus, tram, subway (Metro) or train, you must
purchase the appropriate ticket in advance. In addition to ticket
counters, newsstands are a convenient way to obtain them. Be
prepared to stand in line. It is wise to buy a bigger quantity
than that required for a single trip. Tickets do not expire unless
they are used. The passenger is responsible to validate them upon
boarding the vehicle by using a hole-punching device. Occasional-
ly, a controller will ask to see your ticket. Anyone traveling
without a valid ticket will be fined.

Metro is the fastest way to get around. Three major lines make
most points of the city accessible. You can change directions at
several major stations. Cars leave at three minute intervals.
Millions of people use this system every day.

For longer distances, you may choose to travel by train. One
company, the Hungarian State Railways (MÁV), handles all railroad
transportation. Any location of the country can be reached by
routes originating from the three Union Stations in Budapest.
Their names, Eastern (Keleti), Western (Nyugati) and Southern
(Déli) Union Stations do not express their location in the city but
the destination of the trains leaving from there. Purchase your
ticket in advance. Round trip tickets are more economical. You
have a choice between first and second class cars. It is a good
idea to bring your own drinks and snacks for the trip, as service
is not reliable. However, the vendor going from car to car, sells
good espresso coffee. There are "express" routes to most major
cities that do not stop in small towns and villages. These are
equipped with meal cars that serve tasty and reasonably priced

food. You may decide to leave the country by train. Hungary is well connected to other countries by railways. You are required to make reservations in advance. International trains are usually equipped with sleeping cars.

None of the previously mentioned methods of transportation are air-conditioned except international trains.

b. Taxi

If you would prefer a more comfortable and versatile method of transportation, hire a taxi. Fares might vary: therefore, ask for an estimate in advance. One of the advantages of a cab over a rented car is the freedom from the hassle of finding a parking place. This can be very difficult, especially in the capital. There are several companies offering this service. The list in Budapest includes:

Carrier	Telephone Number
Főtaxi	122-2222
Volán Taxi	166-6666
Buda Taxi	129-4000
City Taxi	153-3633.

c. Car Rental

If you have an international driver's license, you may decide to rent a car. You may do so at any travel agency, Ibusz, Volán or Főtaxi location. You can choose from Eastern or Western European models equipped with standard transmissions. You have the option to hire a driver.

d. Gasoline

In order to fill your rented car with gasoline, consider the following. Gas is sold by the liter. One US gallon equals 3.78 liters. There are fewer service stations than in the United States. They are usually attendant-served and you are expected to tip the attendant.

Fuel is classified as follows: 98 refers to Extra, 92 refers to Super, 86 refers to Normal and K stands for Keverék (Mix). Make sure that you buy the right mixture for your car. The three major gas stations are Áfor, Agip and Shell.

e. Traffic rules

There are slight differences in traffic rules, as well. You are not permitted to make a right turn on red under any circumstance. The rule of right-of-way is very strictly enforced at intersections. You can not make a left turn at major intersections unless there is a traffic light. Speed limit is marked in kilometer/hour. The limits are 120 on highways, 100 on roads, not classified as highways which lie outside of a residential area and 60 km/h on roads located within residential areas. These limits, however, may be overridden by other posted speed limits.

Drunk driving is taken very seriously by the authorities. There is not an allowable blood alcohol content level. If you test positive for any amount of alcohol, your driver's license may be confiscated on the spot. Watch out for pedestrians, as they have the right-of-way over vehicles in many instances.

In the case of an emergency, dial 07 for the police, 05 for the fire department and 04 for the ambulance service.

3. CURRENCY

The official Hungarian currency is the Forint. One Forint equals 100 fillérs. You can exchange your foreign currency or traveler's checks to Forints at the Hungarian National Bank, at the National Savings Register, at most travel agencies and some hotels.

You may use certain major credit cards at certain hotels, shops, department stores and restaurants. Keep your receipts as you may have to show them to the custom officials upon leaving the country. It is considered illegal; however, some street vendors might offer a lot more than the official exchange rate for your hard currency. Be careful not to engage in such transactions. Plan in advance how much of your dollars you want to exchange for Forints. When your journey is over and you want to exchange Forints back to dollars, keep in mind that you are only allowed to get back up to $100. Your passport is required for this transaction.

4. SHOPPING

a. Food

You might be surprised to find out that Hungarian stores generally close much earlier then you may be accustomed to. Most grocery stores are open from 7 AM to 6 PM, or in some instances, until 8 PM. Retail stores are open from 9 AM or 10 AM to 6 PM. Most stores have "Shopping Thursdays", when they stay open till 8 PM. On Saturdays, stores close at 1 PM. These times may vary slightly from store to store. Stores are closed on Sundays and holidays (see Holidays).

You probably will not have to do your own grocery shopping while in the country, but you will soon notice the lack of supermarkets. There are only a few in Budapest and even fewer that offer 24 hour service. If you lived there and decided to have your friends over for dinner, for example, you would have to make several stops in different stores to get everything on your shopping list. From the grocery store, you would go to the meat market. You might not be able to find the kind of meat you wanted, in other words, the selection is limited. Meat is not prepackaged. Price is marked by

the kilo. Bring a bag or basket to carry home your purchased
goods, few places provide bags for your convenience. To get fresh
vegetables and fruit, your way will lead to the market. The
earlier it is in the day, the fresher the produce. Prices vary
throughout the market. It is best to do comparison shopping. Keep
in mind the season of the year. Do not expect strawberries in the
spring, winter or fall. On the other hand, bananas and citrus
fruits are sold in the winter time only. Fresh tomatoes and bell
peppers are a true sign of August. Try the bakery store for bread,
croissants and rolls. It will be delicious but very different from
what you are used to in packaging, size, selection and taste, as
well. Small specialty stores like a deli, a liquor store or a
cukrászda (sweet shop) are the delight of the western tourists.
Everything is sold by the metric unit of measure: 1 kilogram equals
2.2 lbs., 1 meter equals 3.3 feet and 1 liter equals .26 Gallon.

b. Apparel

When shopping for clothes, it is handy to know the European sizes.
A woman size 10 in America is approximately a European size 40, a
shoe size 7 is a 37 in Hungary. A man shoe size 9 is a European
size 42. You can find world class stores and boutiques on Váci
Street in the heart of Budapest. These stores can compete with the
finest in Europe if one seeks quality clothing, jewelry, make-up or
just a small souvenir. Some boutiques carry dresses that are very
fashionable and reasonable priced; however, their purchase may not
be a good investment. Clothes made of cheap material may fade
after the first dry cleaning or washing cycle. In any case, prices
include the tax, which is already calculated.

c. Duty-free shops

There are duty-free shops in the country where goods are only sold
for convertible currency. In stores like these, you may find
bargains if you are interested in folk-art, hand-made wood carving,
embroidery, pottery, etc. These stores can be found in major
hotels, at vital tourist centers (e.g., Lake Balaton) and at
border-crossing points.

When purchasing any electrical appliances, one must know that in
Hungary the standard voltage is 220. An adapter is required for an
electrical device designed for 110 Volts to be operational and vice
versa.

5. RESTAURANT

Hungarians like to go out, but in recent times, they had to cut
back. The main reason is economics. The average Hungarian can not
afford this luxury as often as his American counterpart. Nonethe-
less, you can find a wide variety of restaurants to choose from in
terms of ambiance, yet few from a non-Hungarian cuisine standpoint.
Do not expect to find Japanese, Chinese or any other kind of exotic
restaurants in great numbers.

You are seldom required to make reservations in advance and you do not have to wait to be seated. Very few restaurants have separate smoking and non-smoking sections.

It is not customary to serve iced water. Your cold drinks are pre-chilled and seldom served with ice cubes. Alcohol is served to anyone over the age of 18. Vine is produced in several provinces of the country. Try some of the famous red vine of Eger, the Bull's Blood (Egri Bikavér). One of the finest white vines is the Tokaji Aszu. Pálinka is a Hungarian specialty drink made of plum, apricot or cherries. This is a brandy-like drink with high alcohol content. The beer selection includes domestic and imported beer, as well.

There are no vegetarian plates or salad bars. The salad usually comes with the main course. The salad dressing is a lot different, too. The main meal is served around noon. It consist of three courses. Soup is offered as an appetizer, followed by the main course (usually a meat dish). Your salad is served with this course. Next, indulge yourself in a delicious pastry dessert or ice cream. Espresso coffee is served after the meal. There is no decaffeinated coffee. When you settle your bill, please include your tip. Do not leave it on the table.

Let's list a few things you may find on the menu:

> levesek - soups
> előételek - hors-d'oeuvre
> frissen sültek - meat dishes
> hal ételek - fish dishes
> köretek - side dishes
> saláták - salads
> desszertek - desserts

When the food arrives, it is customary to say "Jó étvágyat!" (good appetite) before one starts eating. The proper way to use your utensils is a little different from the American way. Hold your knife in the right hand and the fork in your left hand throughout the meal. Cut one biteful of food at a time. Don't chop it up in advance and then switch your fork to your right hand in order to eat.

6. RECREATION

Going on a trip does not mean giving up your exercise routine. Many hotels have tennis courts. Such facilities are better than trying to find an expensive court off of the hotel's premises. You can easily find inexpensive swimming pools. Hungary is famous for its health spas. There are numerous spas in the capital including the world famous Gellért Fürdő, as well as in various parts of the country (Harkány, Zalakaros, Hévíz, etc).

While staying in Budapest, jogging is recommended in parks or on the Margit Sziget (Margaret Island) and in the Városliget (City Park). Riding a bike might be dangerous due to heavy traffic and narrow streets, but feel free to enjoy it in rural areas where conditions are better suited for this activity.

The number one sport in the country is soccer. There are many professional clubs and tournaments with different classifications. Every major city has a multi-purpose stadium to accommodate this game. Children get exposed to sports at an early age. Club memberships are very reasonably priced. There is a wide selection of activities to choose from (soccer, handball, volleyball, water polo, tennis, track and field, fencing, etc.) for the youngsters.

Recently, Hungary became one of the host countries for Forma 1 auto racing. Dirt bike racing, mountain climbing, hot air ballooning, cave exploring and gliding are also popular among young people.

The mountains in Hungary cannot be compared to such ranges as the Rocky Mountains from the standpoints of skiing activities and heights. However, hiking in these mountains is a wonderful way of relaxation and, due to the small size of the country, one can enjoy the beauty and fresh air within a short time after leaving the city-life behind.

7. INTRODUCTION/FAREWELLS

Greetings in this country are much more formal and more guided by rules than in America. This is partly due to the differences in the two languages. As is the case with most modern languages, the speaker can address someone in a respectful manner through the appropriate choice of words regarding age, social rank and certain situations. This also applies to greetings.

You may greet a younger person or someone you know very well in an **informal** way. The following words simultaneously express the equivalent of the English "Hi" and "Bye" words: **Szia, Szervusz, Hello.**

A more **formal** way of greeting is to use the time of the day. This is also the safe alternative when one is not sure whether or not an informal greeting is appropriate.

Jó reggelt!	– Good morning.
Jó napot!	– Good day.
Jó estét!	– Good evening.
Jó éjszakát!	– Good night.

The word **"Viszontlátásra!"** is to express good-bye. It is also equivalent to the expression "See you soon".

You may hear children address an older person with the expression **"Csókolom"**. This word doesn't have an English equivalent.

There is an old-fashioned formal greeting form for a gentleman to greet a lady. This might seem odd to an American visitor. The phrase is **"Kezét csókolom!"** (its literal translation means "I kiss your hand"); and at the same time, he may reach for the lady's hand and gently kiss it.

There are rules for introduction, as well. It is customary to introduce a younger person to an older person, a lady to a gentleman and a subordinate to a superior. The same applies when a handshake is called for. In these situations, please keep in mind the fact that the Hungarian language is one of the very few where the family name is used first, followed by the given name.

8. VISITING

When someone invites you over for lunch or dinner, try to be on time. Do not arrive any later than 10-15 minutes. It is not polite to come empty handed. Flowers, candy or a bottle of wine is desirable to bring along. During the visit, if your glass is empty, it may be refilled without asking for permission. To avoid a situation where you have to refuse your refills, you may want to take small sips. If you don't want to drink alcohol at all, you may ask for a soft drink.

9. COMMUNICATIONS

You have to learn not to take everything for granted. Many things are not just a phone call away in this country. Many households are not yet equipped with a telephone. Public phones operate by the insertion of a coin. Operators are not available on a 24-hour basis. The best way to call overseas is via a calling card, by using a public "red phone" or to make your call from the Post Office. In case you decide to choose a public phone, have plenty of change with you. Direct dial is available to most countries. Fax machines can be found at larger hotels and at major Post Offices.

There are newspapers written in English and some radio stations broadcast news in English, as well.

10. CLEANERS

"Patyolat" is the name of the company which offers dry cleaning and laundry services. Express or normal service is available all over the country.

11. HOLIDAYS

There are six national holidays per year. All offices, schools and shops are closed on these days.

As is the case all over the world, **January 1** is a holiday.   This
day follows the biggest party night of the year.

Since the beginning of recent political changes in Eastern Europe,
the **March 15th** celebration again became a symbol of freedom.   On
March 15, 1848 the revolution for freedom started in Budapest on
the steps of the Hungarian National Museum, where the great
Hungarian poet, Sándor Petőfi, recited his poem, the Nemzeti Dal
(National Song).   This revolution was the prelude to a two year
long war against the Habsburgs. The war was defeated with the help
of the Russian Czar. In memory of all the heroes of this revolution and the fight for freedom, this day became a national holiday.
In the past few years its significance grew, as national pride is
no longer suppressed by Russian influence.

Easter Monday is celebrated in this country.   Children do know
about the Easter Bunny, who brings decorated eggs and candy.
According to a folk custom, the boys have to "water" (sprinkle
cologne) on the girls to keep them fresh. First, they have to ask
the girl's permission in a poem.   In return, the girls give them
decorated eggs.

May 1 is May Day. Its significance grew smaller since the dissolu-
tion of communism.

On **August 20**, the country celebrates its constitution.   This is
also the day of King St. István (Stephen) and the celebration of
New Bread. The biggest celebration takes place in the Capital, on
the Danube River with a day-long parade and huge fire works at
night.

October 23 is celebrated in memory of the 1956 Revolution.   This
day has been a holiday only since 1990. This is one more sign of
the changing times in this country.

December 25 & 26 are the Christmas holidays. A tree is decorated
on December 24. Gift-giving takes place on Christmas Eve.   Many
people attend the midnight mass on December 24.   A stronger
religious meaning of this holiday is resurfacing since the
relaxation of communism.

12. TIME/CALENDARS

Hungary is in the Central European time zone.   Time differences
compared to Budapest include:

New York: -6 hours   London: -1 hours   Los Angeles: -9 hours.

Hungary uses daylight saving time from the end of March until the
end of September.

The week starts with Monday. The following is an example of a few
expressions/words in connection with the calendar:

Days of the week:

Hétfő - Monday
Kedd - Tuesday
Szerda - Wednesday
Csütörtök - Thursday
Péntek - Friday
Szombat - Saturday
Vasárnap - Sunday

November - November

Months of the year:

Január - January
Február - February
Március - March
Április - April
Május - May
Június - June
Július - July
Augusztus - August
Szeptember - September
Október - October

December - December

Asking for time: Hány óra van? What time is it?

Quarter past eight - **Negyed** kilenc
Half past eight - **Fél** kilenc
Quarter to nine - **Háromnegyed** kilenc

Time of the day:
reggel - morning
délelőtt - morning (before noon)
dél - noon
délután - afternoon
este - evening
éjjel - night

23

THE HUNGARIAN LANGUAGE

Hungarian belongs to the Finno-Ugric language family, a group which includes both Finnish and Estonian, as well as several other lesser known languages. Although for over a thousand years established in Europe and subjected to the influence of Indo-European and Turkic languages, Hungarian (or **magyar** as it is known in Hungarian) has retained its Finno-Ugric characteristics.

Hungarian is spoken by approximately 16 million people around the world. In addition to the 10 million speakers residing in Hungary, another two million speakers live in Transylvania (western Romania), and another four million are scattered mainly around Europe, North America and Australia.

Just as the other Finno-Ugric languages, Hungarian is an agglutinating language. This means that Hungarian adds suffixes onto the ends of the words which in non-agglutinating languages would be represented by separate words. In the noun, such endings include the possessive suffixes and locative or grammatical cases. A representative example of this would be the word **zsebemben**, "in my pocket". Here the word **zseb**, "pocket" is followed by the suffixes **-em**, "my" and **-ben**, "in".

In the verb, two kinds of conjugations are employed (the definite and the indefinite ones) to mark the presence or absence, respectively, of a definite or third person direct object. An example of this is **látok egy házat**, "I see a house", and **látom a házat**, "I see the house". In addition to adding personal suffixes, the verb may also receive other suffixes denoting possibility, frequentity and/or causativity. For example, **beszél**, "she/he speaks", **beszélget**, "she/he chats" or **beszélgethet**, "she/he may chat".

Some other features of Finno-Ugric languages that Hungarian maintains are the absence of the verb "to have" and the lack of gender distinction. Possession is expressed by the verb "to be" with the object possessed bearing a possessive suffix and the possessor in the dative case. For example, **nekem könyvem van**, "I have a book", literally translated is "to me book-my is".

Another characteristic of Hungarian grammar is the use of postpositions as opposed to prepositions. For example, **a ház mögött**, "behind the house", where **mögött** is the postposition "behind".

Hungarian employs a phenomenon known as vowel harmony. By this it is meant that only front or back vowels can occur in any one word. The front vowels of Hungarian are: **ü**, **ű**, **ö**, **ő** and **e**. The back vowels are **u**, **ú**, **o**, **ó**, **a** and **á**. The vowels, **i**, **í** and **é** are neutral and can occur in words consisting of either front or back vowels. Suffixes, too, come in either back or front vowel varieties and the appropriate suffix must then be added to maintain the vowel harmony of the word. Finally, distinction in length of vowels is maintained in speech and orthography and is indicated by a long mark.

LANGUAGE LESSONS

CONSONANTS

By and large, the consonants in Hungarian are pronounced as in English. All consonants are pronounced. Some consonants are written with two letters (digraphs). The following are the consonants pronounced differently than in English.

c	**ts** as in ca**ts**	**c**ukor	(sugar)
cs	**ch** as in **ch**urch	bo**cs**ánat	(excuse me)
g	always hard as in **g**o	i**g**en	(yes)
gy	similar to a **dj** sound as in **d**uring	ma**gy**ar	(Hungarian)
j	**y** as in **y**es	**j**ó	(good)
ly	**y** as in **y**es	szemé**ly**	(person)
ny	**ny** as in ca**ny**on	ke**ny**ér	(bread)
r	trilling the tongue on top of the mouth	ké**r**em	(please)
s	**sh** as in **sh**e	e**s**te	(evening)
sz	**s** as in **s**at	**sz**ervu**sz**	(hi)
ty	similar to a **tj** sound as in s**t**udio	kár**ty**a	(card)
zs	similar to a **su** sound as in mea**su**re	gará**zs**	(garage)

All consonants can be long or short. Great care should be paid to differences in length; it could change the meaning of a word. Long consonants are written as double consonants and are pronounced two or three times longer than short ones. Length of digraphs is written by doubling the **first** consonant of the digraph. For example, a long **sz** is written **ssz**: vi**ssz**a.

VOWELS

Vowels can be either long or short. Length in the vowels is marked by long marks over the vowel. For example, i vs. í:

i	**e** as in h**e**	mi	(what)

26

í	a longer version of the above, as **ee** in green	tíz	(ten)
e	**a** as in b**a**t	reggel	(morning)
é	**ay** as in s**ay**	kérem	(please)
u	**oo** as in f**oo**d	tud	(know)
ú	a longer version of the above	út	(road)
o	**oh** as in n**o**te	kívánok	(I wish)
ó	a longer version of the above	jó	(good)
a	**aw** as in **aw**l	nap	(day)
á	**aa** as in b**aa**	ár	(price)
ü	the closest English sound is **ew** as in f**ew**	üveg	(bottle)
ű	a longer version of the above	egyszerű	(simple)
ö	as **i** in g**i**rl	köszönöm	(thank you)
ő	a longer version of the above	hétfő	(Monday)

The first syllable of every word is stressed.

ELSŐ LECKE

ISMERKEDÉS / BEMUTATKOZÁS

A repülőgépen

A New Yorkból Budapestre tartó repülőgépen két házaspár ugyanabban a sorban ül.

József: Bocsánat, ez nem az ön szemüvege? Épp most esett le.

Éva: Köszönöm. Szerencse, hogy nem törött el.

József: Először utazik Budapestre?

Éva: Nem. Látogatóba megyünk vissza. 35 éve Amerikában élünk.

Eszter: Vannak még Magyarországon rokonaik?

Zoltán: Nincsenek. Üzleti úton vagyunk és szeretnénk többet látni az országból. Engedjék meg, hogy bemutatkozzam, Koós Zoltán vagyok és a feleségem, Éva.

József: Simon József vagyok és ő a feleségem, Eszter. Mi Budapesten lakunk. Látogatóban voltunk Amerikában.

Éva: Ön mivel foglalkozik?

József: Eszter tanár, én pedig orvos vagyok. És önök?

Zoltán: Éva egy bankban dolgozik, én meg komputereket adok el a fiammal. Önöknek van gyerekük?

Eszter: Igen, egy fiú és egy lány. Általános iskolába járnak. Most a nagymama vigyáz rájuk. Biztosan várnak minket a repülőtéren.

Éva: Nézzék, már szállunk is le!

LESSON ONE

MEETING PEOPLE / INTRODUCTION

On the Airplane

On the plane from New York to Budapest, two couples are sitting in the same row.

József: Excuse me, are these your glasses? They just fell down.

Éva: Thanks. What luck that they didn't break!

József: Is this your first trip to Budapest?

Éva: No, we are going back to visit after 35 years in America.

Eszter: Do you still have relatives in Hungary?

Zoltán: No, we don't. We are on a business trip, but we'd like to see more of the country. My name is Zoltán Koós and this is my wife, Éva.

József: I'm József Simon and this is my wife, Eszter. We live in Budapest. We were visiting America.

Éva: What do you do for a living?

József: Eszter is a teacher and I am a doctor. How about you?

Zoltán: Éva works in a bank and I sell computers with my son. Do you have any children?

Eszter: Yes, a son and a daughter. They go to elementary school. Their grandmother is taking care of them now. I'm sure they are waiting for us at the airport.

Éva: Look, we are already landing!

első	first	feleség	wife
lecke	lesson	ő	he/she
ismerkedés	getting acquainted	mi	we
bemutatkozás	introduction	lakik	live
a	the	mi	what
tart	go to	foglalkozik	be employed in
repülőgép	airplane	tanár	teacher
két	two	én	I
házaspár	couple	pedig	but
ugyanaz	same	orvos	physician
sor	row	egy	a, one
ül	sit	bank	bank
József	Joseph	dolgozik	work
ez	this	komputer	computer
nem	no	elad	sell
az	the, that	fia	son
ön	you (polite address)	gyerek	child
szemüveg	glasses	igen	yes
épp	just	fiú	boy
most	now	lány	girl
leesik	fall off	általános	general
Éva	Eve	iskola	school
szerencse	luck	jár	go to
hogy	that	nagymama	grandmother
eltörik	break	vigyáz	take care of
először	for the first time	biztosan	surely
utazik	travel	vár	wait
látogat	visit	repülőtér	airport
visszamegy	return	néz	look at
év	year	már	already
él	live	leszáll	land
Eszter	Esther	is	also
vannak	(they) are	étel	food
még	still	játék	game, toy
rokon	relative	jókedv	good mood
Magyarország	Hungary	könyv	book
Zoltán	<masculine name>	szék	chair
üzlet	business	ablak	window
vagyunk	(we) are	autó	car
és	and	lámpa	lamp
lát	see	ház	house
több	more	folyó	river
ország	country	száll	fly (v)
enged	let, allow	szükség	need
vagyok	(I) am	asszony	woman

EXPRESSIONS

Bocsánat!	Excuse me!
Köszönöm.	Thank you.
Szeretne látni...	She/he would like to see...
Nincs/nincsenek...	There is no/are no...
Engedje meg, hogy bemutatkozzam.	Let me introduce myself.

GRAMMAR

Hungarian is an agglutinative language, which means that the grammatical informations are carried by suffixes added to the end of the words, unlike in English where prepositions are used in front of the words.

$$szemüveg - glasses$$
$$szemüvegem - \textbf{my glasses}$$

A. Vowel harmony

According to the position of the tongue, the Hungarian vowels can be front or back vowels.

front	short:	e	i	ö	ü
	long:	é	í	ő	ű
back	short:	a	o	u	
	long:	á	ó	ú	

Everybody who learns this language should memorize them because in the Hungarian language vowels have harmony. This means that if the base word is a back vowel word, the suffix should have a back vowel, too. Therefore, there are two different forms for every suffix: one with a front vowel and one with a back vowel.

Examples:

back vowels: **ország** + **ból**   country + from
                           országból   from the country

front vowels: **étel** + **ből**   food + from
                           ételből   from the food

Sometimes the two kinds of vowels are mixed in the same word. In this case the word is a back vowel word.

                játék + **ban**   game + in
                játékban   in the game

In compound words the vowel of the last element determines whether the suffix has a front or back vowel.

                jó + **kedv** + **ben**   good + mood + in
                jókedvben   in good mood

B. Articles

In Hungarian, as well as in English, there are two different kinds of articles:

1. Definite **- a** used before words beginning with a **consonant.**

(THE)
    a könyv - the book
    a szék - the chair

    - az used before words beginning with a **vowel.**

    az ablak - the window
    az autó - the car

2. Indefinite - egy Hungarian language does not use the indefinite article as often as it is required in English. When the object is   **(A)** indefinite, no article is used.

    Mi ez?   - What is this?
    Lámpa.   - It's a lamp.

C. The demonstrative pronouns

ez - this   **Ez** ház.   -   This is a house.
az - that   **Az** folyó. -   That is a river.

The form **"az"** is identical to the definite article **"az"**. The difference between them is the following: the demonstrative pronoun is always stressed, while the article never is.

Az az ablak, **ez** az autó. - **That** is the window, **this** is the car.

Exercises

1. State which class of vowels (front or back) each of the following words belongs to:

jön, ország, Budapest, iskolás, száll, foglalkozás, szükség

2. Use the correct definite article.

...... asszony, ... feleség, ... üzlet, ... tanár,
...... orvos, ... nagymama, ... repülőtér

3. Memorize the conversation in the text. Try to introduce yourself.

MÁSODIK LECKE

VÁMVIZSGÁLAT

Megérkezés Budapestre

<u>Útlevél</u>

József: Itt lehet felvenni a bőröndöket és ott ellenőrzik az útleveleket.

Zoltán: Köszönöm.

Vámtiszt: Jó reggelt! Kérem az útleveleiket! Önöknek magyar nevük van. Beszélik még a nyelvet?

Zoltán: Természetesen. Itt születtünk.

Vámtiszt: Mennyi ideig és hol fognak tartózkodni?

Éva: Két hétig a Fórum Hotelban.

Vámtiszt: Köszönöm szépen, kérem fáradjanak a vámvizsgálathoz.

<u>Vám</u>

Vámtiszt: Jó reggelt! Van valami elvámolni valójuk?

Zoltán: Nincs, csak apró ajándékokat hoztunk.

Vámtiszt: Szeretném látni ezt a bőröndöt. Kinyitná, kérem?

Zoltán: Természetesen, parancsoljon.

Vámtiszt: Minden rendben van, köszönöm. Jó nyaralást kívánok. A viszontlátásra!

34

LESSON TWO

CUSTOMS

Arriving in Budapest

Passport

József: You can pick up your luggage over here and over there is the passport control.

Zoltán: Thank you.

Officer: Good morning. May I see your passports please? You have Hungarian names. Do you still speak the language?

Zoltán: Of course, we were born here.

Officer: How long will you be here and where are you staying?

Éva: We will be staying at the Fórum Hotel for two weeks.

Officer: Thank you very much. Please go on to customs.

Customs

Officer: Good morning. Do you have anything to declare?

Zoltán: No, we brought only small gifts.

Officer: I'd like to see this suitcase. Could you open it for me please?

Zoltán: Of course, here you are.

Officer: Everything is all right, thank you. Have a nice vacation here. Good bye!

VOCABULARY

második	second	csak	only	
vámvizsgálat	customs examination	apró	small, tiny	
megérkezés	arrival	ajándék	gift	
útlevél	passport	hoz	bring	
itt	here	kinyit	open	
lehet	possible	minden	everything	
felvesz	pick up	rend	order	
bőrönd	luggage	nyaralás	vacation	
ott	there	kíván	wish	
ellenőriz	check	nő	woman	
vámtiszt	customs officer	ruha	clothes	
jó	good	este	evening	
reggel	morning	csomag	package, parcel	
kér	ask for	szép	nice	
magyar	Hungarian	asztal	table	
nev	name	ajtó	door	
beszél	speak	te	you	
nyelv	language	ti	you (plural)	
természetesen	of course	ők	they	
születik	be born	posta	post office	
mennyi	how many, how much	busz	bus	
idő	time	villamos	tram	
hol	where	metro	subway	
tartózkodik	stay at	vonat	train	
hét	week	taxi	taxi, cab	
vám	customs	amerikai	American	turis
valami	something	ta	tourist	
elvámol	declare			

EXPRESSIONS

Jó reggelt!	Good morning!
Mennyi ideig?	For how long?
Kérem...	Please...
Köszönöm szépen.	Thank you very much.
Kérem fáradjon a...	Please go to the...
Parancsoljon.	Here you go.
Viszontlátásra!	Good bye!

GRAMMAR

A. **The Accusative Suffix and the Plural Suffix for Nouns, Adjectives and Adverbs**

The **accusative suffix** is **t**.

In Hungarian the direct object of the verb requires this suffix, unlike in the English language which does not have an accusative suffix. The word order subject-verb-object expresses it.

    Látom a fiút.   I can see the boy.

The **plural suffix** is **k**.

    gyerek - gyereke**k**   child - children

In words ending in a vowel, the plural or the accusative suffix is added directly to the word.

    fiú - fiú**t** - fiú**k**   boy   - boys
    nő - nő**t** - nő**k**   woman - women

Words ending in the short vowels **-a**, **-e**, lengthen and change into long vowels **-á**, **-é**.

    ruh**a** - ruh**á**k   clothes
    est**e** - est**é**t   evening

Words ending in a consonant require a linking vowel before these kinds of suffixes according to the rule of vowel harmony. The linking vowel is the same before the accusative suffix (-t) and before the plural suffix (-k).

    csomag - csomag**o**t   -   csomag**o**k   -   package
    útlevél - útlevel**e**t -   útlevel**e**k   -   passport
    szép   - szép**e**t   -   szép**e**k   -   nice

When you use the accusative and the plural suffixes together, the plural suffix always precedes the accusative suffix. In this case the linking vowel can be different.

    csomag -   csomag**okat**   package - packages
    útlevél -   útlevel**eket**   passport - passports

B. **Agreement of the Subject and the Predicate**

The predicate agrees with the subject in number and person.

    Ez asztal.   This is a table.
    Eze**k** asztalo**k**.   These are tables.

37

```
Az ajtó.                    That is a door.
Azok ajtók.                 Those are doors.
```

C.   The Personal Pronouns

	singular	plural
1st person	**én** - I	**mi** - we
2nd person	**te** - you	**ti** - you
3rd person	**ő** - he/she	**ők** - they

Pronouns are used infrequently in Hungarian because the
conjugation of the verb shows who is doing the action.

D.   Present tense of the verb "to be" /lenni/

```
(én)  orvos    vagyok   -    I am a doctor
(te)  orvos    vagy     -    You are a doctor
(ő)   orvos             -    He/she is a doctor
(mi)  orvosok  vagyunk  -    We are doctors
(ti)  orvosok  vagytok  -    You are doctors
(ők)  orvosok           -    They are doctors
```

The sentences clearly show that in third person the singular
and plural forms of the verb "to be" (van, vannak) is always
omitted in present tense in a simple subject sentence.

The negative forms of **van, vannak** are **nincs, nincsenek.**

```
Itt van a posta?        Is the post office here?
Nincs itt.              It is not here.
```

Exercises

1.   Underline the words which have accusative suffix in the text.

2.   Form the plural of the following words:

      busz, villamos, metro, vonat, taxi

3.   In the following sentences fill in the correct form of the
      verb "to be".

      Mi magyarok .... Ti amerikaiak ....? Ők orvosok
      .... Te tanár ....? Ó turista ....

HARMADIK LECKE

KÖZLEKEDÉS

Taxi

Simonék találkoznak a gyerekekkel és a nagymamával a kijáratnál.

Lány: Milyen volt a repülőút, Anyu?

Eszter: Nagyon jó. Megismerkedtünk egy kedves házaspárral a gépen. Nemsokára ti is látni fogjátok őket mert eljönnek vacsorázni a jövő héten.

József: Induljunk haza. Ott egy taxiállomás.

Sofőr: Jó reggelt! Hova szeretnének menni?

József: A XII. kerület Hegyalja utca 282-be. Tudja hol van?

Sofőr: Igen, Budán. Szerintem két autóra lesz szükségük. Túl sok a csomag és különben sem fér öt ember egy kocsiba.

József: Rendben van. Eszter, te menj a gyerekekkel. Otthon találkozunk.

József: Szerencse hogy nem volt nagy forgalom. Álljon meg itt kérem, ez a mi házunk. Mennyit fizetek?

Sofőr: Az óra 724 Forintot mutat.

József: Tessék, itt van 800 Forint. A többi az öné. Kaphatnék egy nyugtát róla?

Sofőr: Igen...

József: Köszönöm, viszontlátásra!

LESSON THREE

LOCAL TRANSPORTATION

Taxi

The Simons meet their children and their grandmother at the exit.

Girl: How was your flight, Mom?

Eszter: It was perfect. We met a nice couple on the airplane. You'll see them soon because they will come to dinner next week.

József: Let's go home. There is a cabstand.

Driver: Good morning. Where would you like to go?

József: 282 Hegyalja Street, in the XII. district. Do you know where it is?

Driver: Yes, in Buda. I think you will need two cars. You have too much luggage and five people can't fit in one car.

József: It's all right. Eszter, you go with the kids. See you at home.

József: We were lucky that the traffic was very light. Please stop here, this is our house. How much is it?

Driver: The meter reads 724 Forint.

József: Here you are, 800 Forint. Keep the change. Could you please give me a receipt?

Driver: Yes.

József: Thank you. Good bye!

harmadik	third	túl	too (much)
közlekedés	transportation	sok	many, much
találkozik	meet sy	különben	besides
kijárat	exit	sem	neither
milyen	what kind	fér	fit into
volt	was	öt	five
repülőút	flight	ember	person, man
anyu	mother	kocsi	car
nagyon	very	otthon	at home
kedves	dear, nice	szerencsés	lucky
gép	plane, machine	nagy	big
nemsokára	soon	forgalom	traffic
mert	because	megáll	stop
eljön	come	fizet	pay
vacsora	dinner	óra	meter, clock
jövő	next, future	mutat	show
indul	start	kap	get, receive
haza	home	nyugta	receipt
taxiállomás	cabstand	olvas	read
sofőr	driver	ír	write
hova	where to	ért	understand
megy	go	vesz	take
kerület	district	ad	give
utca	street	számla	bill
tud	know	maga	you (polite address)
szerint	according to	áll	stand

EXPRESSIONS

Induljunk haza.	Let's go home.
Rendben van.	It's all right.
Otthon találkozunk.	See you at home.
Tessék.	Here you go.
A többi az öné.	Keep the change.

GRAMMAR

A. The infinitive

The infinitive is formed by adding the suffix **-ni** to the base verb.

olvas - **ni**	**to** read
ír - **ni**	**to** write

B. Conjugation

There are two sets of suffixes for the two kinds of conjugation in the Hungarian language: the definite and the indefinite one.

1. The **Definite Conjugation** is used when a definite object is preceded by the definite article **a, az**.

Olvasom **a** könyvet.   I read **the** book.

	back vowel verb	front vowel verb
én	tud - **om**	ért - **em**
te	tud - **od**	ért - **ed**
ő	tud - **ja**	ért - **i**
mi	tud - **juk**	ért - **jük**
ti	tud - **játok**	ért - **itek**
ők	tud -**ják**	ért - **ik**

When the base verb ends in **s**, **z** or **sz**, we double these instead of using the j suffix.

olva**s**	+ **j**uk	=	olva**ss**uk
ho**z**	+ **j**a	=	ho**zz**a
ve**sz**	+ **j**ük	=	ve**ssz**ük

2. The **Indefinite Conjugation** is used when there is no object, or an indefinite one only.

Egy könyvet olvasok.   I read **a** book.

	back vowel verb	front vowel verb
én	vár - **ok**	kér - **ek**
te	vár - **sz**	kér - **sz**
ő	vár - -	kér - -
mi	vár - **unk**	kér - **ünk**
ti	vár - **tok**	kér - **tek**
ők	vár - **nak**	kér - **nek**

C. **The polite form of address**

The polite form of address is expressed by the third person.

Ön - Maga   you - in singular
Önök - Maguk   you - in plural

Ön beszél magyarul?   Do you speak Hungarian?
Maguk amerikaiak?   Are you Americans?

An alternative form is the use of **tetszik** (singular)/**tetszenek** (plural) followed by the infinitive of the verb.

Hogy tetszik lenni?   How are you?
Mit tetszenek kérni?   What do you want?

Exercises

1. Add the personal suffixes to the following verbs.

(ők) Találkoz..... a gyerekekkel.
(ti) Lát..... a taxit.
(mi) Kér..... két kocsit.
(én) Ad..... a számlát.

2. Give the number, person and conjugation of the following verbs.

tudod, állnak, szeretem, olvassák

3. Try to translate the English text back to Hungarian.

NEGYEDIK LECKE

SZÁLLÁS

Hotel

Koósék megérkeznek a Fórum Hotelba.

Zoltán: Jó reggelt! Koós Zoltán vagyok. Egy kétágyas szobát foglaltam New York-ból.

Portás: Igen uram. Kérem töltse ki ezeket a papirokat... Köszönöm. Itt a kulcs. A 312-es szoba az önöké, a harmadik emeleten. A lift jobbra van, a lépcső mellett. A bőröndök azonnal a szobájukban lesznek.

Zoltán: Hol parkolhatunk az autóval?

Portás: A hotel földalatti parkolójában.

Éva: Meg tudná mondani, hogy mikor és hol kaphatunk reggelit? Úgy hallottam, hogy ez benne van az árban.

Portás: Az étteremben a bárral szemben. Ott lehet reggelizni reggel 7-től 10-ig. De a szobapincéri szolgálatot is igénybe vehetik.

Éva: Még milyen szolgáltatásaik vannak?

Portás: Itt a földszinten van fodrász, ajándék bolt és pénzváltó hely. Az alagsorban van az úszómedence és a kondicionáló terem. Ha bármire szükségük lenne, kérem szóljanak.

LESSON FOUR

ACCOMMODATIONS

Hotel

Mr. and Mrs. Koós just arrived at the Fórum Hotel.

Zoltán: Good Morning. My name is Zoltán Koós. I reserved a room for two from New York.

Clerk: Yes sir. Please fill out these forms. Thank you. Here is the key. Your room number is 312. It is on the third floor. The elevator is on the right, next to the stairs. Your luggage will be in your room immediately.

Zoltán: Where can we park the car?

Clerk: In the hotel's underground parking lot.

Éva: Could you tell me when and where we can have breakfast? I've heard that it's included in the price.

Clerk: Yes, in the restaurant across from the bar. You can have breakfast there from 7 a.m. to 10 a.m. But you can also ask for room service.

Éva: What other kind of services do you offer?

Clerk: Here on the first floor we have a hair dresser, a gift shop and a money-exchange counter. The swimming pool and the health club are in the basement. If you need anything else, please let us know.

VOCABULARY

negyedik	fourth	ár	price	
szállás	accommodation	étterem	restaurant	
hotel	hotel	bár	bar	
megérkezik	arrive	szemben	opposite to	
kétágyas szoba	double room	reggelizik	have breakfast	
foglal	reserve	de	but	
portás	front desk clerk	szobapincér	room service	
uram	sir (salutation)	waiter		
kitölt	fill out	szolgálat	service	
papir	paper	igénybe vesz	take advantage of	
kulcs	key	földszint	first floor	
emelet	floor	fodrász	hairdresser	
lift	elevator	bolt	shop	
jobb	right	pénzváltó	money-changer	
lépcső	stairway	hely	place	
mellett	next to, by	úszómedence	swimming pool	
azonnal	right away	kondicionáló terem	workout room	
parkol	park sg	alagsor	basement	
földalatti	underground	ha	if	
parkoló	parking lot	bármi	anything	
megmond	say, tell	szól	speak, say, talk	
mikor	when	jön	come	
reggeli	breakfast	eszik	eat	
úgy	so, that	iszik	drink sg	
hall	hear	alszik	sleep	
benne	in, inside	vacsorázik	have dinner	
benne van	included in sg	alma	apple	

EXPRESSIONS

Meg tudná mondani...	Can you tell me...
Úgy hallottam...	I heard that...
Kérem szóljanak, ha...	Please ask, if...

GRAMMAR

A. Irregular Verbs

The following two verbs have only an indefinite conjugation:

jön - come   megy - go

én	megyek	jövök
te	mész	jössz
ő	megy	jön
mi	megyünk	jövünk
ti	mentek	jöttök
ők	mennek	jönnek

B. -ik Verbs

Some Hungarian verbs end in -ik in the third person singular of the present tense. The indefinite conjugation rule applies to them.

eszik, iszik, alszik, dolgozik, vacsorázik, etc.

Most -ik verbs have only an indefinite conjugation form, exceptions are: eszik, iszik.

C. Verbal Prefixes

Verbal prefixes modify the verb's original meaning and often give it a figurative sense. The most commonly used ones are:

be	-	into	bemegy	-	go into
ki	-	out of, from	kimegy	-	go out
le	-	down	lemegy	-	go down
fel	-	up	felmegy	-	go up
el	-	away, from	elmegy	-	go away
át	-	across	átmegy	-	go across
rá	-	onto	rámegy	-	go onto
vissza	-	back	visszamegy	-	go back

There are two prefixes which usually express the completion of an action.

meg   Zoltán eszi az almát.   Zoltán is eating the apple.
        Zoltán megeszi az almát. Zoltán has eaten the apple.

el   Éva olvassa a könyvet.   Éva is reading the book.

Éva elolvassa a könyvet. Éva has read the book.

The prefixes usually stay in front of the verb.

> Bejön a szobába.
> Megírja a levelet.

But sometimes the prefix should be separated from the verb and placed after it, when the stress is on any other part of the sentence, not on the prefix.

> Én megyek el.
> Nem jövünk be.
> Mikor hozod el?

Exercises

1. Underline the verbs with suffixes in the text.

2. Fill in the blanks using the correct personal suffixes.

   Én .... dolgozni.   (menni)
   Ti .... haza.   (jönni)
   Ők .... a reggelit.   (megenni)
   Ő otthon ....   (vacsorázni)

3. Translate the English text into Hungarian.

ÖTÖDIK LECKE

ÚTBAIGAZÍTÁS

A postára menet

Koósék levelet szeretnének feladni.

Éva: Bocsánat. Meg tudná mondani, hogy hol találhatjuk a legközelebbi postát?

Járókelő: Igen, gyalog is közel van. Menjenek egyenesen ezen az utcán az első lámpáig. Ott forduljanak balra és a második sarkon jobbra. A posta a harmadik épület. De a 6-os villamost is használhatják. Az első megálló a múzeum. A második egy nagy áruház. Ott szálljanak le és éppen a posta előtt lesznek.

Éva: Köszönöm.

A postán

Zoltán: Jó napot kívánok! Levelet szeretnénk küldeni Amerikába.

Hivatalnok: Kérem, menjenek a harmadik ablakhoz. Itt csak csomagot lehet feladni.

Zoltán: Mennyibe kerül ez a két levél légi postával New York-ba?

Hivatalnok: Először meg kell mérnem. 132 Forint.

Zoltán: Köszönöm. Hány nap alatt érnek oda?

Hivatalnok: Körülbelül egy hét alatt.

Éva: Köszönjük. Viszontlátásra!

LESSON FIVE

ASKING FOR DIRECTIONS

Going to the Post Office

Mr. and Mrs. Koós would like to send letters home.

Éva: Excuse me. Could you tell me where the nearest post office is?

Pedestrian: Yes, it is within walking distance. Go straight down this street until the first light. Turn left and at the second corner, turn right. The post office is the third building. But you can also take the #6 tram. The first stop is the Museum. The second is a big supermarket. Get off there and you will be right in front of the Post Office.

Éva: Thank you.

At the Post Office

Zoltán: Good afternoon. We'd like to send these letters to America.

Clerk #1.   Please go to the third window. This is for packages only.

Zoltán: How much does it cost to send these letters by air mail to New York?

Clerk #2:   I have to weigh them first. It's 132 Forint.

Zoltán: Thank you. In how many days will they get there?

Clerk #2:   Approximately in a week.

Éva: Thanks. Good bye.

VOCABULARY

ötödik	fifth	hivatalnok	clerk
menet	on the way	légi posta	air mail
levél	letter	kell	must (do sg)
felad	mail sg	mér	weigh
legközelebbi	nearest	odaér	arrive at, reach
járókelő	pedestrian	körülbelül	approximately
gyalog	on foot	honnan	where from
közel	near, not far	szálloda	hotel
egyenesen	straight ahead	ki	who
lámpa	light	vagy	or
fordul	turn	kicsi	small
bal	left	szekrény	cupboard
sarok	corner	bokor	bush, shrub
épület	building	fa	tree
használ	use	gyár	factory
megálló	(bus) stop	kert	garden
múzeum	museum	színház	theater
áruház	department store	táska	bag
leszáll	get off	mesél	tell a story
éppen	just, exactly	híd	bridge
előtt	in front of	város	city, town
küld	send		

EXPRESSIONS

Útbaigazítás kérés. Asking for directions.

GRAMMAR

A. Adverbs of Place

1. Hungarian has no prepositions. English prepositions are translated by suffixes. The most important suffixes relating to space can show:

1.	movement towards a position	– **HOVÁ?** (where to)
2.	state of rest	– **HOL?** (where)
3.	movement away from a position	– **HONNAN?** (where from)

	HOVÁ?	HOL?	HONNAN?
inside	-ba, -be into	-ban, -ben in, at	-ből, -ből from, out of
surface	-ra, -re onto	-n, -on, -en, -ön on	-ról, -ről from
point in space, proximity	-hoz, -hez, -höz to	-nál, -nél at	-tól, -től (away) from

A szállodá**hoz** megyek.	I am going **to** the hotel.
A szállodá**nál** várlak.	I wait for you **at** the hotel.
A szállodá**tól** jövök.	I am coming **from** the hotel.

The use of place suffixes is often combined with the use of verbal prefixes in order to express direction.

Bemegyek a szobá**ba.**	I am going **into** the room.
A szobá**ban** vagyok.	I am **in** the room.
Kijövök a szobá**ból.**	I come **out of** the room.

Felszállok a villamos**ra.**	I get **onto** the tram.
Ülök a villamos**on.**	I am sitting **on** the tram.
Leszállok a villamos**ról.**	I get **off** the tram.

2. The suffixes of the adverb of place can be added to the interrogatives **ki** and **mi**.

Kinél vacsorázol?	**At whom** do you have dinner?
Miből veszed?	**From what** do you buy it?

3. These suffixes can also be added to the demonstrative pronouns **ez, az**. In this case the **z** of the pronoun assimilates with the first consonant of the suffix.

ez + be = **ebbe**   az + ba = **abba**

```
ez + re  = erre            az + ra  = arra
ez + nél = ennél           az + nál = annál
ez + hez = ehhez           az + hoz = ahhoz
ez + től = ettől           az + tól = attól        ETC.
```

B. Conjunctions

és   - and   Éva **és** Zoltán olvas.
               Éva **and** Zoltán are reading.

vagy - or   Este tévézek **vagy** levelet írok.
               In the evening I watch TV **or** write a letter.
de   - but   Fáradt vagyok, **de** elmegyek.
               I'm tired **but** I'll go.

nem ... hanem   A szoba **nem** nagy, **hanem** kicsi.
               The room **isn't** large, **but** small.

hanem can only be used following a clause containing the word
nem.

C. Postpositions

Postpositions always directly follow the noun to which they
refer.

```
alatt    - under            Az asztal alatt...
fölött   - above            A szekrény fölött...
előtt    - in front of      A ház előtt...
mögött   - behind           A bokor mögött...
mellett  - beside, next to  A hotel mellett...
között   - between          A fák között...
körül    - around           Az iskola körül...
```

Exercises

1. Answer the questions, using the appropriate suffixes to
express

        (a) a point in space:
        Example: Hová mész?   A gyárhoz megyek.
                                    (kert, színház, múzeum)

        (b) surface:
        Example: Hol van a levél? A táskán.
                                    (asztal, könyv, posta)

        (c) inside:
        Example: Honnan jössz?   A hotelból jövök.
                                    (bolt, Amerika, ház)

```
```

2. Insert a demonstrative pronoun in the following sentence and provide the appropriate suffixes.

Example:
A házban lakik.   (ez)   Ebben a házban lakik.

A könyvről mesél. (az)
A hídtól jövök.   (ez)
A városba megyek. (az)

3. Memorize the directions in Hungarian from the text.

HATODIK LECKE

SZÓRAKOZÁS

Az Étteremben

Zoltán: Jó estét kívánok! Simon névre foglaltunk asztalt négy személyre.

Pincér: Jó estét! Kérem kövessenek. Ez az asztal megfelel?

Zoltán: Sajnálom, de ez túl közel van a zenekarhoz. Szeretem a cigányzenét, de attól tartok, hogy beszélgetéshez ez túl hangos.

Pincér: Ez a csendes sarok jobb lenne?

Zoltán: Igen, köszönöm.

Pincér: Mit szeretnének inni?

Eszter: Én egy száraz Martinit kérek.

Éva: Én is.

József: Koós úr, megkóstolna egy magyar italt? Én barack pálinkát kérek. Nem tart velem?

Zoltán: De, miért ne?

Pincér: Parancsoljanak, az étlapok. Amíg átnézik, hozom az italokat.

Eszter: Éva! Zoltán! Miért magázódunk? Tegezzük egymást.

Éva: Jó, ez sokkal könnyebb barátok között. Egészségünkre!

Együtt: Egészségünkre!

Pincér: Elkészültek a rendeléssel?

Éva: Igen. Én halászlét és csirke-paprikást szeretnék uborka salátával.

Eszter: Én bablevest és rántott-sajtot rizzsel.

Zoltán: Én húslevest és töltött-paprikát kérek.

József:	Én pedig hagymás-rostélyost sült-krumplival.
Pincér:	Ajánlhatok valami jó magyar bort a vacsorához? Az Egri Bikavér száraz vörösbor, míg a Tokaji Furmint édesebb fehér.
Zoltán:	Bikavért kérünk.
Pincér:	Köszönöm.

Megérkezik az étel, mindenki enni kezd.

József:	Hogy érzitek magatokat itthon?
Éva:	Nagyon jól. Budapest sokat változott, alig ismertünk rá.
Zoltán:	Nagyon sok szép helyet láttunk sétáink alatt. Itt nem szeretünk vezetni, mert nagyon nehéz parkolni és a forgalom is nagy.
Eszter:	Ezért járunk mi metróval vagy villamossal. Csak a hétvégén vezetünk ha elmegyünk a városból.
Pincér:	Hogy ízlett a vacsora?
Zoltán:	Finom volt.
Éva:	Már régóta nem ettem ilyen jót.
Pincér:	Parancsolnak kávét vagy édességet?
Zoltán:	Nem, köszönjük. Fizetni szeretnénk.

A pincér hozza a számlát. Zoltán kifizeti és borravalót ad a pincérnek.

LESSON SIX

GOING OUT

At the Restaurant

Zoltán: Good evening! We have reservations for four under the name of Simon.

Waiter: Good evening! Please follow me! Would this table be suitable for you?

Zoltán: I am sorry, but it is too close to the band. I like gypsy music, but I'm afraid it will be too loud for conversation.

Waiter: Would this quiet corner be better?

Zoltán: Yes, thank you.

Waiter: What would you like to drink?

Eszter: I would like to have a dry Martini.

Éva: I will have one, too.

József: Mr. Koós, would you like to taste a Hungarian drink? I will have apricot brandy. Would you care to join me?

Zoltán: Sure, why not!

Waiter: Here are the menu cards. While you take a look at them, I will bring your drinks.

Eszter: Éva! Zoltán! Why are we so formal? Why don't you call us Eszter and József?

Éva: All right. It's a lot easier among friends. Cheers!

All: Cheers!

Waiter: Are you ready to order?

Éva: Yes, I would like to have fish soup, chicken-paprikás with cucumber salad.

Eszter: I would like to eat bean soup and breaded cheese with rice.

Zoltán: I would like to order meat soup and stuffed peppers.

József: I will have a stewed cutlet with fried potatoes.

Waiter: May I suggest some good Hungarian wine with your dinner? Bull's Blood is a dry red wine, while Tokaji Furmint is a sweeter white one.

Zoltán: We will have the Bull's Blood.

Waiter: Thank you.

The food arrives and everybody starts to eat.

József: How do you feel being back home?

Éva: Very much. Budapest has changed a lot, we could hardly recognize it.

Zoltán: We saw many beautiful places during our walks. We don't like to drive here because it's so difficult to park and the traffic is so heavy.

Eszter: That's why we ride the subway and the tram. We only drive if we leave town on the weekends.

Waiter: How did you like your dinner?

Zoltán: It was delicious.

Éva: I haven't had such good food for a long time.

Waiter: Would you like some dessert or coffee?

Zoltán: No, thank you. We would like the check, please.

The waiter brings the bill. Zoltán pays it and gives a tip to the waiter.

hatodik	sixth		rizs	rice
szórakozás	entertainment		húsleves	meat soup
	(going out)		töltött-paprika	stuffed peppers
négy	four		hagymás-rostélyos	stewed cutlet
személy	person		sült-krumpli	fried potatoes
pincér	waiter		ajánl	suggest
követ	follow		bor	wine
megfelel	be suitable		vörös	red
zene	music		míg	while
zenekar	band		édes	sweet
szeret	like, love		édesebb	sweeter
cigányzene	gypsy music		fehér	white
beszélgetés	conversation		mindenki	everybody
hangos	loud		kezd	start, begin
csendes	quiet		itthon	at home
jobb	better		változik	change
száraz	dry		alig	hardly
úr	Sir, mister		ráismer	recognize
megkóstol	taste		séta	walk
ital	drink		alatt	during
barack	peach		vezet	drive
pálinka	brandy like drink		nehéz	hard
étlap	menu card		ezért	that is why
amíg	while		metró	subway
átnéz	look through		hétvége	week-end
miért	why		elmegy	leave
egymást	each other		finom	delicious, fine
barát	friend		régóta	long (since)
között	between, among		ilyen	such
együtt	together		kávé	coffee
elkészül	get ready		édesség	sweets
rendelés	order		kifizet	pay
halászlé	fish soup		borravaló	tip
csirke-paprikás	chicken-paprikás		játszik	play
uborka saláta	cucumber salad		fut	run
bableves	bean soup		akar	want
rántott-sajt	breaded cheese			

59

EXPRESSIONS

Jó estét kívánok.	Good Evening.
Sajnálom.	I am sorry.
Attól tartok, hogy...	I am afraid that...
Nem tart velem?	Would you care to join me?
Miért ne?	Why not!
Átnézni valamit.	To take a look at something.
Miért **magázódunk**[3]?	
Tegezzük[4] egymást!	
Egészségünkre!	Cheers!
Hogy ízlett[5] a vacsora?	How did you like your dinner?

Magázódás is the word to describe the "polite form of address" (discussed in the Grammar section of Lesson Three) in Hungarian. It is a formal manner of expression that indicates respect and distance among the speakers. This form of address is very common in many languages; however, there is no equivalent manner of expression in the English Language.

Tegeződés is an informal way of addressing one another. It expresses a more intimate relationship among the speakers (e.g., friendship, close acquaintance). It is like a small ceremony when one initiates the switch from "magázódás" to "tegeződés" and makes it official with a drink.

This verb usually pertains to food.

GRAMMAR

A. The past tense

Hungarian has only one past tense.   All the English past tenses are translated by this single one.

The past tense is formed by adding **-t** or **-tt** to the present tense stern.

The short suffix **-t** is added directly to the verb base when this ends in a consonant.

beszél - beszélt

vár - vá**rt**

The long suffix **-tt** requires a linking vowel, and it is used:

1.   when a verb ends in two consonants

já**tsz**(ik):   já**tsz** + **o** + **tt**   =   játszott

2.   when a verb ends in t

fut: fut + **o** + **tt**   =   futott

B. The personal suffixes of the past tense

In the past tense, like in the present tense, there are two kinds of conjugations: the definite and the indefinite ones.

1. Definite conjugation

	beszél + t	fut + ott
én	beszélt - **em**	futott - **am**
te	beszélt - **ed**	futott - **ad**
ő	beszélt - **e**	futott - **a**
mi	beszélt - **ük**	futott - **uk**
ti	beszélt - **étek**	futott - **átok**
ők	beszélt - **ék**	futott - **ák**

2. Indefinite conjugation

	beszél + t	fut + ott
én	beszélt - **em**	futott - **am**
te	beszélt - **él**	futott - **ál**
ő	beszélt - -	futott - -
mi	beszélt - **ünk**	futott - **unk**
ti	beszélt - **etek**	futott - **atok**
ők	beszélt - **ek**	futott - **ak**

C. The past tense of the verb "to be"

én	voltam	mi	voltunk
te	voltál	ti	voltatok
ő	volt	ők	voltak

Otthon voltak ma este.   They were at home tonight.

D. The past tense of the irregular verbs: jönni, menni

én	jöttem	mentem
te	jöttél	mentél
ő	jött	ment
mi	jöttünk	mentünk
ti	jöttetek	mentetek
ők	jöttek	mentek

E. The numeral

The numeral is generally used as an attribute and takes no endings in this case. Nouns preceded by a numeral are always singular.

```
két gyerek        two children

sok asztal        lots of tables
```

sok   -   many, much, a lot of
Sok barátom van.   I have **lots of** friends.

kevés -   few
Csak **kevés** ember jött.   Only a **few** people came.

néhány -   some
Ismerek **néhány** jó boltot.   I know some good stores.

minden -   all, every
Mindenki jól van.   **Everybody** is well.

```
 1 - egy      11 - tizenegy          40 - negyven
 2 - kettő/két 12 - tizenkettő       50 - ötven
 3 - három                           60 - hatvan
 4 - négy     20 - húsz              70 - hetven
 5 - öt       21 - húszonegy         80 - nyolcvan
 6 - hat      22 - húszonkettő       90 - kilencven
 7 - hét                            100 - száz
 8 - nyolc    30 - harminc          400 - négyszáz
 9 - kilenc   31 - harmincegy      1000 - ezer
10 - tíz      32 - harminckettő     5000 - ötezer
```

1992 ezerkilencszázkilencvenkettő

Exercises

1. Underline the verbs in past tense in the text.

2. Practice the use of past tense in the following sentences.

    Hogy érzitek magatokat?   Metroval járunk dolgozni.
    Zoli akar fizetni.   Én halászlét kérek.

3. Read these numbers in Hungarian.
    5, 28, 2, 1989, 12

4. Memorize from the text how to order in a restaurant.

63

HETEDIK LECKE

VÁSÁRLÁS

Egy Áruházban

Éva és Zoltán a Luxus áruházba akarnak menni vásárolni.

Éva: Siess, Zoltán! Az áruház 6 órakor bezár és ha elkésünk, csak holnap mehetünk vissza 10 óra után.

Éva: Jó napot kívánunk! Egy nyári öltönyt szeretnénk venni a férjemnek.

1. Eladó: Hányas a mérete, uram?

Zoltán: 40-es vagy 42-es, nem vagyok benne biztos.

1. Eladó: Ebben a méretben van fehér, drapp vagy világoskék.

Zoltán: Szürkében nincs?

1. Eladó: De van, de az lehet hogy kicsi önnek. Szeretné felpróbálni? Ott van a próbafülke.

Zoltán: Köszönöm. Tökéletes. Mennyibe kerül?

1. Eladó: 13,200 Forint.

Zoltán: Tessék.

Éva: Meg tudná mondani, hogy hol a cipő osztály?

1. Eladó: Ott, pontosan a háta mögött.

2. Eladó: Segíthetek?

Éva: Egy szép magas sarkú cipőt szeretnék 38-as méretben.

2. Eladó: Ott vannak azon a két polcon.

Éva: Köszönöm. Ezt szeretném felpróbálni.

2. Eladó: Sajnálom, de ez nincs az ön méretében. Talán a jövő héten lesz.

Éva: Köszönöm. Majd visszajövök.

LESSON SEVEN

SHOPPING

In a Department Store

Éva and Zoltán want to go to the Luxus store to shop.

Éva: Hurry, Zoltán! The store will close at 6 p.m. and if we're late, we have to go back tomorrow after 10 in the morning.

Éva: Good afternoon. We would like to buy a summer suit for my husband.

Clerk #1: What is your size, Sir?

Zoltán: 40 or 42, I am not sure.

Clerk #1: In those sizes we have white, beige or light blue.

Zoltán: Do you have them in gray, too?

Clerk #1: Yes, we do, but it might be too small for you. Would you like to try it on? The fitting room is over there.

Zoltán: Thank you. It's just perfect. How much is it?

Clerk #1: 13,200 Forint.

Zoltán: Here you are.

Éva: Could you tell us where the shoe department is?

Clerk #1: There, right behind you.

Clerk #2: May I help you?

Éva: I would like a nice pair of high-heeled shoes in size 38.

Clerk #2: There are some on those two shelves.

Éva: Thank you. I'd like to try these on.

Clerk #2: I'm sorry, but we don't have them in your size. Maybe next week we will.

Éva: Thank you. I'll be back.

VOCABULARY

hetedik	seventh	világoskék	light blue
vásárlás	shopping	szürke	grey
vásárol	shop sg	felpróbál	try on
siet	hurry	próbafülke	fitting room
óra	clock	tökéletes	perfect
bezár	close	cipő	shoes
elkésik	be late	cipő osztály	shoe department
holnap	tomorrow	pontosan	exactly
után	after	hát	back
nyár	summer	mögött	behind
öltöny	suit	segít	help
férj	husband	polc	shelf
eladó	clerk	visszajön	return, come back
méret	size	elutazik	go on a trip, travel
drapp	beige		

EXTRA WORDS

Ruházat	**Clothing**	**Színek**	**Colors**
ing	shirt	piros	red
bluz	blouse	sárga	yellow
trikó	T-shirt	zöld	green
nadrág	pants, trousers	kék	blue
szoknya	skirt	narancssárga	orange
ruha	dress	lila	purple
zokni	socks	fekete	black
harisnya	panty hose	barna	brown
kabát	coat	sötétkék	dark blue
köntös	robe	rózsaszín	pink
fehérnemű	underwear		
papucs	slippers		
magas sarkú cipő	high-heeled shoes		
csizma	boots		

Élelmiszer	**Groceries**	**Gyümölcs**	**Fruit**
kenyér	bread	körte	pear
tej	milk	szilva	plum
vaj	butter	szőlő	grapes
felvágott	cold cuts	narancs	orange
sonka	ham	dinnye	water melon
sajt	cheese	eper	strawberries
szalonna	bacon		
tojás	eggs		
zsemle	roll		

Zöldség	**Vegetable**		
paradicsom	tomato		
paprika	bell pepper		
saláta	lettuce		hagym
a	onion		

EXPRESSIONS

Az áruház **6 órakor** bezár.	The department store closes **at 6 o'clock.**
Hányas a méreted?	What is your size?
Nem vagyok benne biztos.	I'm not sure.
Mennyibe kerül?	How much does it cost?
Segíthetek?	May I help you?

GRAMMAR

A. The future tense

1. To express future tense in Hungarian the auxiliary verb **fog** is used followed by the infinitive form of the verb.

   Nem fogok enni vacsorát.   I won't eat dinner.
   Mikor fogsz megérkezni?   When will you arrive?

   The definite and indefinite conjugation of the verb **fog** is the same as any other back vowel verb's.

2. In Hungarian the present tense can be used to express future action when the time is specified.

   Holnap megyünk vásárolni.   We'll go shopping tomorrow.
   A jövő héten utazok el.   I'll go on a trip next week.

3. Future tense is frequently expressed by the adverb **majd**.

   Majd meglátjuk.   We will see.
   Majd este átmegyek.   I'll go over tonight.

B. Future tense of the verb "to be"

The future tense of the verb "to be" is expressed by the present tense of the verb **lenni**.

én	leszek	mi	leszünk
te	leszel	ti	lesztek
ő	lesz	ők	lesznek

Mikor **lesztek** otthon?   When **will you be** home?

Reggel iskolában **leszek**. I **will be** in school in the morning.

C. Interrogatives

As you will see, the Hungarian interrogatives are as simple as the English but some of them have plural forms, too.

Ki - who	**Ki** ez?	**Who** is this?
Kik - who	**Kik** ezek?	**Who** are these?

Mi - what	**Mi** az?	**What** is that?
Mik - what	**Mik** azok?	**What** are those?

Melyik - which one
Melyek - which ones

Melyik házat vetted meg?	**Which** house did you buy?
Melyek tetszenek neked?	**Which ones** do you like?

Milyen   - what is (it) like
              - what kind of
Milyenek - what are (these) like
              - what kinds of

Milyen öltönyt szeretne?   **What kind of** suit do you want?
Milyenek a boltok Budapesten? **What** are the stores **like** in Budapest?

Hol - where

Hol lakik Éva?	**Where** does Éva live?

Honnan - where form

Honnan érkezik a vonat?	**Where** is the train arriving from?

Hová - where (to)

Hová mész?	**Where** are you going?

Mikor - when

Mikor látlak?	**When** will I see you?

Hány	- how many
Mennyi	- how much

69

Hány gyereked van?	**How many** kids do you have?
Mennyi pénzed van?	**How much** money do you have?

Miért - why, how come

Miért nem eszel?   **Why** don't you eat?

Hogy - how

Hogy vagy?   **How** are you?

Exercises

1. Conjugate the verb **fog** in both conjugations.

2. Change the following sentences to express future action.

    András ma érkezik.   Fehér cipőt veszek.   Zoltán öltönyt
    próbál.   Miért nem jöttök át?

3. Describe a visit to the grocery store using the extra words
    from the vocabulary.

NYOLCADIK LECKE

VENDÉGSÉGBEN

Vacsora meghívás

Éva:	Simonék meghívtak minket vacsorázni ma estére.
Zoltán:	Milyen kedves tőlük. Hány órára?
Éva:	Hétre. Korábban kéne elindulnunk, mert még ajándékot kell nekik vásárolni.
Zoltán:	Mit szeretnél venni?
Éva:	Virágot, egy üveg bort és egy kis csokit a gyerekeknek. Siess, indulnunk kell egy óra múlva.

Simonéknál csengetnek.

Eszter:	Itt van Éva és Zoltán. Nyiss ajtót légy szíves!
József:	Sziasztok! Gyertek be! Nehezen találtatok ide?
Zoltán:	Nem, könnyen mert taxival jöttünk. Tessék, virág a ház asszonyának és neked egy üveg bor. Hol vannak a gyerekek?
Eszter:	A nagymamánál. Jaj, de gyönyörű ez a virág! Köszönöm szépen.
József:	Mit isztok? Gint vagy vodkát?
Éva:	Én gint kérek tonikkal.
Zoltán:	Én is.
József:	Nézzetek körül. A lakás nem nagy, de nagyon kényelmes. Erre vannak a hálószobák és a fürdőszoba. A konyha a nappaliból nyílik.
Zoltán:	Valaminek nagyon jó illata van. Mi az?
Eszter:	Hagyományos magyar vacsorát főztem: Hortobágyi palacsinta előételnek, aztán húsleves, rántott hús, töltött káposzta és rétes.
Éva:	De Eszter, ez túl sok! Ennyit egy hét alatt sem szoktunk enni.

71

Eszter: Majd meglátjuk.

Vacsora után.

Zoltán: Rengeteget ettem, de minden nagyon finom volt. Köszönöm.

Eszter: Szívesen. Menjünk át a nappaliba.

Éva: Hadd segítsek leszedni az asztalt.

Eszter: Az még várhat, de a pezsgő nem.

Két órával később.

Zoltán: Nagyon késő van. Mennünk kell. Tudnál egy taxit hívni?

József: Természetesen. (Tárcsáz.) Jó estét. Tudna küldeni egy taxit a XII. kerület Hegyalja utca 282-be, Simon névre? A telefon szám 155-5555. Köszönöm. Tíz perc múlva itt lesz.

Éva: Köszönjük ezt a csodálatos estét. Nagyon jól éreztük magunkat. Eszter, holnap felhívlak. Sziasztok.

Eszter és József: Sziasztok! Jó éjszakát!

LESSON EIGHT

BEING A GUEST

Dinner Invitation

Éva: The Simons invited us for dinner tonight.

Zoltán: How nice of them. What time?

Éva: At seven o'clock. We should leave earlier because we need to buy them a gift.

Zoltán: What do you want to buy?

Éva: Flowers, a bottle of wine and some chocolate for the kids. Hurry up, we have to leave in an hour.

At the Simons' home. The bell rings.

Eszter: Éva and Zoltán are here. Open the door, please.

József: Hi! Come in, please. Was it difficult to find our place?

Zoltán: No, it was easy because we took a taxi. Here are some flowers for the lady of the house, and a bottle of wine for you. Where are the kids?

Eszter: They are at grandma's. These flowers are beautiful. Thanks.

József: What would you like to drink? Gin or vodka?

Éva: I will have a gin and tonic please.

Zoltán: Me too.

József: Let me show you around. The apartment isn't big but it's very comfortable. Here are the bedrooms and the bathroom. The kitchen opens off of the living room.

Zoltán: Something smells very good here. What is it?

Eszter: I prepared a traditional Hungarian dinner: pancake á la Hortobágy for appetizer, then meat soup, breaded cutlet, stuffed cabbage and strudel.

Éva: But, Eszter, we can't eat everything. It's even too much for a week.

Eszter: We'll see.

After dinner.

Zoltán: I ate too much, but everything was delicious. Thank you.

Eszter: You're welcome. Let's go to the living room.

Éva: Let me help you clear the table.

Eszter: It can wait, but the champagne can't.

Two hours later.

Zoltán: It's very late. We must go. Could you call a taxi for us, please?

József: Of course. (He dials.) Good evening. Could you send a cab to 282 Hegyalja Street, XII. District under the name of Simon? The phone number is 155-5555. Thank you. It will be here in ten minutes.

Éva: Thanks for the wonderful evening. We really enjoyed your hospitality. Eszter, I'll call you tomorrow. Good bye.

Eszter and József: Bye! Good night!

VOCABULARY

nyolcadik	eighth	fürdőszoba	bathroom
vendégség	being a guest	konyha	kitchen
meghívás	invitation	nappali	living room
ma	today	illat	(pleasant) smell
ma este	this evening	hagyományos	traditional
korábban	earlier	főz	cook
vesz	buy	palacsinta	pancake
virág	flower	előétel	appetizer
üveg	bottle	rántott hús	breaded cutlet
csoki	chocolate	töltött káposzta	stuffed cabbage
csenget	ring the bell	rétes	strudel
nyit	open	pezsgő	champagne
bejön	come in	hív	call
talál	find	tárcsáz	dial
könnyen	easily	telefon szám	telephone number
gyönyörű	beautiful	csodálatos	wonderful
körül	around	felhív	phone sy
lakás	apartment	olcsó	cheap
kényelmes	comfortable	pohár	glass, cup
hálószoba	bedroom		

EXPRESSIONS

Milyen kedves tőlük!	How nice of them!
Egy óra múlva.	Within an hour.
Légy szíves!	Please.
Sziasztok!	Hi!
Majd meglátjuk.	We will see.
Rengeteget ettem.	I ate too much.
Szívesen.	You are welcome.
Leszedi az asztalt.	She clears the table.
Nagyon késő van.	It is very late.
Jó éjszakát!	Good night!

GRAMMAR

A. The Possessive Suffixes

1. The English possessives (my, your, his, etc.) are expressed by suffixes in Hungarian. The suffix is added to the base word when it ends in a vowel. Words ending in a consonant require a linking vowel.

(én)	szobám	lakásom
(te)	szobád	lakásod
(ő)	szobája	lakása
(mi)	szobánk	lakásunk
(ti)	szobátok	lakásotok
(ők)	szobájuk	lakásuk

Az ő szobája nagy.   **His** room is big.
Az én lakásom kicsi.   **My** apartment is small.

2. Plurality of Possession

The sign of the plural possession is the vowel **-i**, placed between the base word and the possessive suffix. There is no possessive suffix in the 3rd person singular and plural.

szobáim	szobáink
szobáid	szobáitok
szobái	szobáik

B. Possessive Relations

When the possessor is known, the possession can be expressed by the suffix **-é**.

Zoltáné - Zoltán's   a lányé - the girl's

The interrogative **KI** can also take the suffix **-é**:

Kié ez a ház?   **Whose** house is this?
Az apámé.   My father's.

Kié ez a gyerek?   **Whose** child is he?
A nővéremé.   My sister's.

C. **The possessive Pronouns**

enyém - mine	miénk - ours
tiéd - yours	tiétek - yours
övé - his, hers	övék - theirs

Ez az autó az **enyém**.   This car is **mine**.
Tiéd ez a könyv vagy az **övé**?   Is this book **yours** or **hers**?

For plurality of possession see the previous page.

Ezek a könyvek a tieid.   These books are **yours**.

D. **Comparison of Adjectives**

The comparative suffix **-bb** is added to the base word.   The superlative is formed by the prefix **leg-** and the comparative suffix **-bb**.

nagy	big	olcsó	cheap
nagy**obb**	bigg**er**	olcs**óbb**	cheap**er**
legnagy**obb**	bigg**est**	**leg**olcs**óbb**	cheap**est**

Irregular forms:

sok	many	szép	nice	kicsi	small
több	more	szebb	nicer	kisebb	smaller
legtöbb	most	legszebb	nicest	legkisebb	smallest

The simplest method of comparing one thing to another is to use the comparative suffix **-bb** and the word **mint** (than).

Az én táskám nehez**ebb**, **mint** a tiéd.   My suitcase is heavi**er than** yours.

Idős**ebb** vagyok **mint** te.   I am old**er than** you.

Exercises

1. Add the proper possessive suffixes to the following words:

   (én) gyerek, (ő) ruha, (mi) barát, (te) lakás, (ti) szoba.

2. Answer the questions with the possessive pronouns:

   Kié ez a szoba? (én) Az enyém.   Whose room is this? Mine.
   Kié ez a pohár? (te)   Whose glass is this?
   Kié ez a sok könyv? (mi)   Whose books are these?

3. Memorize the name of the meals from lessons 6 and 8. Prepare a menu card for a Hungarian dinner.

KILENCEDIK LECKE

ORVOSI VIZSGÁLAT

Betegség

Korán reggel a hotel szobában.

Zoltán: Nem tudom mi bajom van, de szörnyen érzem magam.

Éva: Sápadt vagy. Fáj valamid?

Zoltán: A gyomrom, a fejem és nagyon szédülök.

Éva: Hívom a portát, hogy küldjenek egy orvost.

Megérkezik az orvos.

Orvos: Jó reggelt. Doktor Nagy Péter vagyok. Mi a probléma?

Éva: A férjem nem érzi jól magát.

Orvos: Kérem üljön fel és vegye le a pizsama kabátját. Megmérem a lázát. Egy kis hőemelkedése van, 37.6°C^6. A vérnyomása normális. Hol fáj a gyomra? Itt? Hadd lássam a nyelvét! Köszönöm. Önnek gyomorrontása van. Mit evett tegnap?

Zoltán: Túl sokat. A barátainknál vacsoráztunk.

Orvos: Úgy látszik, már elszokott a magyar konyhától. Nagyon finom, de nehéz a gyomornak. Két napig szigorú diétára van szüksége. Csak tea, piritós, főtt krumpli és holnaputánra rendben lesz. Viszontlátásra.

Zoltán: Köszönöm. Viszontlátásra.

The normal body temperature is 36.5–37.0°C. This is approximately 98.6°F.

78

LESSON NINE

MEDICAL CARE

Being sick

Early morning in the hotel room.

Zoltán: I don't know what's wrong with me, but I feel awful.

Éva: You look very pale. Do you hurt?

Zoltán: I have a stomachache and a headache and I feel very dizzy.

Éva: I call the front desk to ask for a doctor.

The doctor arrives.

Doctor: Good Morning. I'm Doctor Péter Nagy. What is the problem?

Éva: My husband doesn't feel good.

Doctor: Please, sit up and take your pajama top off. Let me take your temperature. You have a slight fever of 37.6°C. Your blood pressure is normal. Where does your stomach hurt? Here? Let me see your tongue, please. Thank you. You have an upset stomach. What did you eat yesterday?

Zoltán: Too much. We had dinner at our friends' house.

Doctor: It seems that you're not used to Hungarian food anymore. It's delicious, but very heavy on the stomach. You need a special diet for two days. Only tea, toast and boiled potatoes and the day after tomorrow you should be fine. Good bye.

Zoltán: Thank you. Good bye.

VOCABULARY

kilencedik	ninth	vérnyomás	blood pressure
orvosi vizsgálat	medical examination	normális	normal
korán	early	nyelv	tongue
szörnyen	awfully	gyomorrontás	upset stomach
sápadt	pale	tegnap	yesterday
fáj	hurt	szigorú	strict
gyomor	stomach	diéta	diet
fej	head	tea	tea
szédül	be dizzy	piritós	toast
porta	front desk	főtt krumpli	boiled potato
probléma	problem	ráz	shake
leül	sit down	öröm	pleasure
levesz	take off	tűnik	appear
pizsama kabát	pajama top	mosolyog	smile
láz	fever	lelkileg	emotionally
hőemelkedés	slight fever	sérült	wounded

EXTRA WORDS

homlok	forehead	vese	kidney
orr	nose	máj	liver
szem	eyes	hugyhólyag	bladder
arc	face	méh	womb
száj	mouth	láb	leg
fül	ear	comb	thigh
mellkas	chest	térd	knee
has	abdomen	boka	ankle
hát	back	kéz	hand
szív	heart	könyök	elbow
tüdő	lungs	csukló	wrist
epe	gallbladder	újj	finger

EXPRESSIONS

Fáj a gyomrom.	I have a stomachache.
Fáj a fejem.	I have a headache.
Megmérem a lázad.	I take your temperature.
Elszokott a magyar konyhától.	He is **not used to** Hungarian food **anymore**.

Meg vagyok fázva.	I have a cold.
Náthás vagyok.	I have the flu.
Köhögök.	I have a cough.
Lázas vagyok.	I have a fever.
Fáj a torkom.	I have a shore throat.
Megrándult a bokám.	I sprained my ankle.
Terhes vagyok.	I am pregnant.

GRAMMAR

A. The imperative (subjunctive) of Verbs

1. The imperative is commonly used in everyday speech to give an order or to make a request.

   Légy jó!   Be good.
   Menjünk haza!   Let's go home.

   The imperative is formed by adding the suffix **-j** to the base verb.

kér - ask for	
Definite	Indefinite
kér**j**em	kér**j**ek
kér**j**ed, kérd*	kér**j**él, kérj*
kér**j**e	kér**j**en
kér**j**ük	kér**j**ünk
kér**j**étek	kér**j**etek
kér**j**ék	kér**j**enek

   *   The second person singular has long and short forms. The short form is more frequently used.

   Kér**j**étek el a könyvet!   **Ask** for the book.

2. The **-j** suffix assimilates with the last consonant of the base verb when it ends in -s, -z or -sz.

   s + j = ss
   Olva**ss**a fel a levelet!   **Read** the letter aloud.

   z + j = zz
   Rá**zz**uk le a fáról!   **Let's shake it** off the
tree.

   sz + j = ssz
   Já**tssz**anak nekünk valamit! They **must play** something
                                   for us.

81

3. The imperative of a few irregular verbs.

van (to be)	megy (go)	jön (come)
legyek	menjek	jöjjek
legyél, légy	menjél, menj	jöjjél, jöjj
legyen	menjen	jöjjön
legyünk	menjünk	jöjjünk
legyetek	menjetek	jöjjetek
legyenek	menjenek	jöjjenek

4. In an imperative sentence the verbal prefix or any other modifier is placed after the verb.

Menjetek **be** a szobába!	Go **into** the room.
Ne késsetek **el**!	Don't be late.
Álljatok **fel** oda!	Stand **up** there.

B. **Adverbs of Manner**

Adverbs of manner can be expressed by flexional suffixes and postpositions.

Suffixes:

-val, -vel **by, with**
Örö**mmel** segített nekem.   He helped me **with** pleasure.

-nak, -nek **as**
Hangos**nak** tűnik.   It appears **as** loud.

-an, -en **-ly**
Kedves**en** mosolyog.   She is gent**ly** smiling.

-lag, -leg **-ly**
Lelki**leg** sérült.   He is emotional**ly** wounded.

-ul, -ül **-ly**
Türelmetlen**ül** vár.   He is waiting impatient**ly**.

Postpositions:

helyett **instead of**
Ő ment **helyett**em.   He went **instead of** me.

nélkül **without**
Nem tudok **nélkül**ed élni.   I can't live **without** you.

82

szerint   according to
Anna **szerint** jó idő lesz.   **According to** Anne, the weather
                               will be nice.

ellen   against
Nem tettem semmit **ellene**.   I did nothing **against** it.

Exercises

1. Underline the imperative verbs in the text.

2. Complete these commands:

   (te) Ül..... le a székre!
   (ő) Megy..... az orvoshoz!
   (mi) Kér..... a magyar könyvet!
   (ti) Vigyáz..... magatokra az úton!

3. Learn the extra words from the vocabulary. Pretend that you
   have the flu. Try to explain it to the doctor.

TIZEDIK LECKE

TÁRSADALMI ÉLET

Koktél-parti

Koósék koktél-partit rendeznek és Simonékat is meghívják.

Zoltán:	Kiss úr, engedje meg, hogy bemutassam magyar barátainkat: Simon József és Eszter a felesége. Kiss Gábor, magyarországi részlegünk igazgatója.
Az igazgató:	Örülök hogy megismertem. Ön is üzletember?
József:	Nem, én orvos vagyok. Már régóta dolgozik Zoltánnal?
Kiss úr:	Nem, még csak két napja írtuk alá a szerződést és a jövő hónapban kezdjük a munkát. Addigra az íratok rendben lesznek.
Zoltán:	Mi az USÁ-ban vásároljuk a komputereket és onnan szállítjuk őket Magyarországra. Az itteni kirendeltségünk készíti a programokat a magyar piac számára.
József:	Biztos vagyok benne, hogy ez remek ötlet. Az időzítés tökéletes, mert erre most itt nagy szükség van. Sok szerencsét.
Eszter:	Későre jár. Mennünk kéne, József korán megy munkába. Köszönjünk a meghívást. Nagyon élveztük a partit.
Éva:	Köszönjük, hogy eljöttetek. Nekünk is korán kell kelnünk. A repülőgép tíz órakor indul és még nem csomagoltunk be.
Zoltán:	Nagyon jól éreztük magunkat veletek. Örülök, hogy megismerkedtünk. Itt a névjegy-kártyám. Ha legközelebb Amerikában jártok, feltétlenül hivjatok fel. Addig is írjatok.
József:	Ti már tudjátok a cimünket és a telefonszámunkat. Mi is várjuk a leveleteket. Jó utat! Vigyázzatok magatokra!

LESSON TEN

SOCIALIZING

At the business party

Mr. and Mrs. Koós give a cocktail party and they invite the Simons, too.

Zoltán: Mr. Kiss, let me introduce our Hungarian friends: József Simon and Eszter, his wife. Gábor Kiss, the director of our Hungarian division.

The Director: Nice to meet you. Are you a businessman, too?

József: No, I am a doctor. Have you been working with Zoltán for a long time?

Mr. Kiss: No, we only signed the contract two days ago and we'll start working together next month. By then we should have finished the paperwork.

Zoltán: We produce the computers in the U.S. and ship them to Hungary. Our division here writes the software for the Hungarian market.

József: I'm sure, it's an excellent idea. The timing is perfect because there is a great need for this here. Good luck!

Eszter: It's getting late. We should be leaving, József has to be at work early. Thanks for inviting us. We really enjoyed the party.

Éva: Thank you for coming. We have to get up early, too. Our plane leaves at 10 a.m. and we haven't packed yet.

Zoltán: We had a great time with you. It's so nice to have met you. Here is my business card. Next time you come to America, please give us a call, by all means. Until then, keep in touch.

József: You already know our address and telephone number. We will also be waiting for your letter. Have a nice trip. Take care of yourselves.

VOCABULARY

tizedik	tenth	program	program
társadalom	society	piac	market
társadalmi élet	social life	remek	magnificent
koktél-parti	cocktail party	ötlet	idea
rendez	organize	időzítés	timing
részleg	division	élvez	enjoy
igazgató	director	felkel	get up
üzletember	businessman	becsomagol	pack
aláír	sign sg	névjegy kártya	business card
szerződés	contract	feltétlenül	by all means
hónap	month	kisbaba	baby
munka	work	mozi	movie theater
irat	document, paperwork	csésze	cup
szállít	ship, transport	víz	water
kirendeltség	division	pénz	money
készít	make, prepare	szülő	parent

EXPRESSIONS

Örülök hogy megismertem.	Nice to meet you.
Komputer programot készít.	He writes computer software.
Sok szerencsét!	Good luck!
Jó utat!	Have a nice trip.
Vigyázzatok magatokra!	Take care of yourselves.

GRAMMAR

A. **The Conditional Mode**

To form the conditional mode of a verb in present tense, add the suffix **-na, -ne, -ná** or **né** to the base word. The personal suffixes are added to this new stem.

szeret-**né-**k   I would like
mutat-**ná-**d   You would show

szeret - like	
Definite	Indefinite
szeret**ném**	szeret**nék**
szeret**néd**	szeret**nél**
szeret**né-**	szeret**ne-**
szeret**nénk**	szeret**nénk**
szeret**nétek**	szeret**nétek**
szeret**nék**	szeret**nének**

mutat - show	
Definite	Indefinite
mutat**nám**	mutat**nék**
mutat**nád**	mutat**nál**
mutat**ná-**	mutat**na-**
mutat**nánk**	mutat**nánk**
mutat**nátok**	mutat**nátok**
mutat**nák**	mutat**nának**

Szeretnénk hazamenni.   We would like to go home.
Megmutatná az utat?   Would you show the way?

87

2. The conditional mode of the verb **lenni** (to be).

én	lennék	mi	lennénk
te	lennél	ti	lennétek
ő	lenne	ők	lennének

3. The conditional mode of some irregular verbs:

	jön (come)	megy (go)
én	jönnék	mennék
te	jönnél	mennél
ő	jönne	menne
mi	jönnénk	mennénk
ti	jönnétek	mennétek
ők	jönnének	mennének

4. The past tense in conditional mode.

To express past tense in conditional mode, the past tense form of the verb is followed by the word **volna**.

Mentem **volna**.	I **would have** gone.
Lettél **volna**.	You **would have** been.

B. **Verbs expressing possibility**

To express possibility, the verb base takes the formative suffix **-hat, -het**.

Megnéz**het**jük a kisbabát? **May** we see the baby?
Me**het**ek moziba? **May** I go to the movie theater?

Verbs formed with the suffix **-hat, -het** take all modes and tenses. They behave in the same manner as a regular verb base when other suffixes are added to it.

Jö**het**ek korábban? **May** I come earlier?

Lát**hat**tad volna hogy jön a busz. You **could** have seen the bus coming.

Kap**hat**nék egy csésze teát? **May** I have a cup of tea?

88

Exercises

1. Form the conditional mode of the verbs in present tense.

   Ha te is (eljön) hozzám, ő is (jön).
   (Megnéz én) a lakásodat.
   Nem (hív te) helyettem fel?

2. Form the verb of possibility from the underlined verbs.

   Kérek egy pohár vizet.
   Van nálam pénz, megveszem ezt a cipőt.
   Ma korán lefekszem.
   Ír levelet a szüleinek.

3. Learn from the text how to say good-bye to your friends.

Lesson 1.

1. front: jön, Budapest, szükség
   back : ország, iskolás, száll, foglalkozás

2. az asszony, a feleség, az üzlet, a tanár, az orvos,
   a nagymama, a repülőtér

Lesson 2.

1. bőröndöket, útleveleket, reggelt, útleveleiket,
   nyelvet, reggelt, ajándékokat, bőröndöt, nyaralást

2. buszok, villamosok, metrok, vonatok, taxik

3. vagyunk, vagytok, -, vagy, -

Lesson 3.

1. találkoznak, látjátok, kérünk, adom

2. tudod   - second person, singular, definite
   állnak   - third person, plural, indefinite
   szeretem   - first person, singular, definite
   olvassák   - third person, plural, definite

Lesson 4.

1. megérkeznek, vagyok, foglaltam, töltse ki,
   köszönöm, lesznek, parkolhatunk, tudna, kaphatunk,
   hallottam, vehetik, vannak, lenne, kérem, szóljanak

2. megyek, jöttök, megeszik, vacsorázik

Lesson 5.

1. kerthez, színházhoz, múzeumhoz
   asztalon, könyvön, postán
   boltból, Amerikából, házból

2. Arról a könyvről mesél.
   Ettől a hídtól jövök.
   Abba a városba megyek.

Lesson 6.

1. foglaltunk, elkészültek, változott, ismertünk rá,
   láttunk, ízlett, volt, ettem

2. Hogy érzitek magatokat?
   Zoli akart fizetni.
   Metroval jártunk dolgozni.

Én halászlét kértem.

3. öt, huszonnyolc, ezerkilencszázcyolcvankilenc,
   tizenkettő

Lesson 7.

1. | Indefinite | Definite |
   |------------|----------|
   | fogok | fogom |
   | fogsz | fogod |
   | fog | fogja |
   | fogunk | fogjuk |
   | fogtok | fogjátok |
   | fognak | fogják |

2. András ma fog érkezni. or András ma érkezik. Fehér
   cipőt fogok venni. Zoltán öltönyt for próbálni.
   Miért nem fogtok átjönni?

Lesson 8.

1. gyerekem, ruhája, barátunk, lakásod, szobájuk

2. A tiéd. A miénk.

Lesson 9.

1. küldjenek, üljön fel, vegye le, lássam

2. ülj, menjen, kérjük, vigyázzatok

Lesson 10.

1. eljönnél, eljönne, megnézném, hívnád

2. kérhetek, megvehetem, lefekhetek, írhat

a (1) the
ablak (1) window
ad (3) give
ajándék (2) gift
ajánl (6) suggest
ajtó (2) door
akar (6) want
alagsor (4) basement
aláír (10) sign sg
alatt (6) during
alig (6) hardly
áll (3) stand
alma (4) apple
alszik (4) sleep
általános (1) general
amerikai (2) American
amíg (6) while
anyu (3) mother
apró (2) small, tiny
ár (4) price
arc (9) face
áruház (5) department store
asszony (1) woman
asztal (2) table
átnéz (6) look through
autó (1) car
az (1) that
az (1) the
azonnal (4) right away
bableves (6) bean soup
bal (5) left
bank (1) bank
bár (4) bar
barack (6) peach
barát (6) friend
bármi (4) anything
barna (7) brown
becsomagol (10) pack
bejön (8) come in
bemutatkozás (1) introduction
benne (4) in, inside
benne van (4) included in sg
beszél (2) speak
beszélgetés (6) conversation
bezár (7) close
biztosan (1) surely
bluz (7) blouse
boka (9) ankle
bokor (5) bush, shrub
bolt (4) shop
bor (6) wine

borravaló (6) tip
bőrönd (2) luggage
busz (2) bus
cigányzene (6) gypsy music
cipő osztály (7) shoe department
cipő (7) shoes
comb (9) thigh
csak (2) only
csendes (6) quiet
csenget (8) ring the bell
csésze (10) cup
csirke-paprikás (6) chicken-paprikás
csizma (7) boots
csodálatos (8) wonderful
csoki (8) chocolate
csomag (2) package, parcel
csukló (9) wrist
de (4) but
diéta (9) diet
dinnye (7) water melon
dolgozik (1) work
drapp (7) beige
édes (6) sweet
édesebb (6) sweeter
édesség (6) sweets
egy (1) a, one
egyenesen (5) straight ahead
egymást (6) each other
együtt (6) together
él (1) live
elad (1) sell
eladó (7) clerk
élelmiszer (7) groceries
eljön (3) come
elkésik (7) be late
elkészül (6) get ready
ellenőriz (2) check
elmegy (6) leave
előétel (8) appetizer
először (1) for the first time
előtt (5) in front of
első (1) first
eltörik (1) break
elutazik (7) go on a trip, travel
elvámol (2) declare
élvez (10) enjoy
ember (3) people
emelet (4) floor
én (1) I
enged (1) let, allow

epe **(9)** gallbladder
eper **(7)** strawberries
épp **(1)** just
éppen **(5)** just, exactly
épület **(5)** building
ért **(3)** understand
és **(1)** and
este **(2)** evening
eszik **(4)** eat
Eszter **(1)** Esther
étel **(1)** food
étlap **(6)** menu
étterem **(4)** restaurant
év **(1)** year
Éva **(1)** Eve
ez **(1)** this
ezért **(6)** that is why
fa **(5)** tree
fáj **(9)** hurt
fehér **(6)** white
fehérnemű **(7)** underwear
fej **(9)** head
fekete **(7)** black
felad **(5)** mail sg
feleség **(1)** wife
felhív **(8)** phone sy
felkel **(10)** get up
felpróbál **(7)** try on
feltétlenül **(10)** by all means
felvágott **(7)** cold cuts
felvesz **(2)** pick up
fér **(3)** fit into
férj **(7)** husband
fia **(1)** son
finom **(6)** delicious, fine
fiú **(1)** boy
fizet **(3)** pay
fodrász **(4)** hairdresser
foglal **(4)** reserve
foglalkozik **(1)** be employed in
folyó **(1)** river
fordul **(5)** turn
forgalom **(3)** traffic
földalatti **(4)** underground
földszint **(4)** first floor
főtt krumpli **(9)** boiled potato
főz **(8)** cook
fül **(9)** ear
fürdőszoba **(8)** bathroom
fut **(6)** run
gép **(3)** plane, machine
gyalog **(5)** on foot
gyár **(5)** factory
gyerek **(1)** child

gyomor **(9)** stomach
gyomorrontás **(9)** upset stomach
gyönyörű **(8)** beautiful
gyümölcs **(7)** fruit
ha **(4)** if
hagyma **(7)** onion
hagymás-rostélyos **(6)** stewed cutlet
hagyományos **(8)** traditional
halászlé **(6)** fish-soup
hall **(4)** hear
hálószoba **(8)** bedroom
hangos **(6)** loud
harisnya **(7)** panty hose
harmadik **(3)** third
has **(9)** abdomen
használ **(5)** use
hát **(7)** back
hatodik **(6)** sixth
ház **(1)** house
haza **(3)** home
házaspár **(1)** couple
hely **(4)** place
hét **(2)** week
hetedik **(7)** seventh
hétvége **(6)** week-end
híd **(5)** bridge
hív **(8)** call
hivatalnok **(5)** clerk
hogy **(1)** that
hol **(2)** where
holnap **(7)** tomorrow
homlok **(9)** forehead
hónap **(10)** month
honnan **(5)** where from
hotel **(4)** hotel
hova **(3)** where to
hoz **(2)** bring
hőemelkedés **(9)** slight fever
hugyhólyag **(9)** bladder
húsleves **(6)** meat soup
idő **(2)** time
időzítés **(10)** timing
igazgató **(10)** director
igen **(1)** yes
igénybe vesz **(4)** take advantage of
illat **(8)** (pleasant) smell
ilyen **(6)** such
indul **(3)** start
ing **(7)** shirt
ír **(3)** write
irat **(10)** document, paperwork
is **(1)** also
iskola **(1)** school
ismerkedés **(1)** getting acquainted

iszik **(4)** drink sg
ital **(6)** drink
itt **(2)** here
itthon **(6)** at home
jár **(1)** go to
járókelő **(5)** pedestrian
játék **(1)** game, toy
játszik **(6)** play
jó **(2)** good
jobb **(6)** better
jobb **(4)** right
jókedv **(1)** good mood
jön **(4)** come
jövő **(3)** next, future
József **(1)** Joseph
kabát **(7)** coat
kap **(3)** get, receive
kávé **(6)** coffee
kedves **(3)** dear, nice
kék **(7)** blue
kell **(5)** must (do sg)
kényelmes **(8)** comfortable
kenyér **(7)** bread
kér **(2)** ask for
kert **(5)** garden
kerület **(3)** district
két **(1)** two
kétágyas szoba **(4)** double room
kéz **(9)** hand
kezd **(6)** start, begin
ki **(5)** who
kicsi **(5)** small
kifizet **(6)** pay
kijárat **(3)** exit
kilencedik **(9)** ninth
kinyit **(2)** open
kirendeltség **(10)** division
kisbaba **(10)** baby
kitölt **(4)** fill out
kíván **(2)** wish
kocsi **(3)** car
koktél-parti **(10)** cocktail party
komputer **(1)** computer
kondicionáló terem **(4)** workout room
konyha **(8)** kitchen
korábban **(8)** earlier
korán **(9)** early
köntös **(7)** robe
könnyen **(8)** easily
könyök **(9)** elbow
könyv **(1)** book
körte **(7)** pear
körül **(8)** around
körülbelül **(5)** approximately

követ **(6)** follow
közel **(5)** near, not far
közlekedés **(3)** transportation
között **(6)** between, among
kulcs **(4)** key
küld **(5)** send
különben **(3)** besides
láb **(9)** leg
lakás **(8)** apartment
lakik **(1)** live
lámpa **(5)** light
lámpa **(1)** lamp
lány **(1)** girl
lát **(1)** see
látogat **(1)** visit
láz **(9)** fever
lecke **(1)** lesson
leesik **(1)** fall off
légi posta **(5)** air mail
legközelebbi **(5)** nearest
lehet **(2)** possible
lelkileg **(9)** emotionally
lépcső **(4)** stairway
leszáll **(1)** land
leszáll **(5)** get off
leül **(9)** sit down
levél **(5)** letter
levesz **(9)** take off
lift **(4)** elevator
lila **(7)** purple
ma **(8)** today
ma este **(8)** this evening
maga **(3)** you (polite address)
magas sarkú cipő **(7)** high-heeled
shoes
magyar **(2)** Hungarian
Magyarország **(1)** Hungary
máj **(9)** liver
már **(1)** already
második **(2)** second
még **(1)** still
megáll **(3)** stop
megálló **(5)** (bus)stop
megérkezés **(2)** arrival
megérkezik **(4)** arrive
megfelel **(6)** be suitable
meghívás **(8)** invitation
megkóstol **(6)** taste
megmond **(4)** say, tell
megy **(3)** go
méh **(9)** womb
mellett **(4)** next to, by
mellkas **(9)** chest
menet **(5)** on the way

mennyi (2) how many, how much
mér (5) weigh
méret (7) size
mert (3) because
mesél (5) tell a story
metro (2) subway
mi (1) what
mi (1) we
miért (6) why
míg (6) while
mikor (4) when
milyen (3) what kind
minden (2) everything
mindenki (6) everybody
mögött (7) behind
mosolyog (9) smile
most (1) now
mozi (10) movie theater
munka (10) work
mutat (3) show
múzeum (5) museum
nadrág (7) pants, trousers
nagy (3) big
nagymama (1) grandmother
nagyon (3) very
nappali (8) living room
narancs (7) orange
narancssárga (7) orange
négy (6) four
negyedik (4) fourth
nehéz (6) hard
nem (1) no
nemsokára (3) soon
név (2) name
névjegy kártya (10) business card
néz (1) look at
nő (2) woman
normális (9) normal
nyár (7) summer
nyaralás (2) vacation
nyelv (9) tongue
nyelv (2) language
nyit (8) open
nyolcadik (8) eighth
nyugta (3) receipt
ő (1) he/she
odaér (5) arrive at, reach
ők (2) they
öl (1) lap
olcsó (8) cheap
öltöny (7) suit
olvas (3) read
ön (1) you (polite address)
óra (7) clock

óra (3) meter, clock
öröm (9) pleasure
orr (9) nose
ország (1) country
orvos (1) physician
öt (3) five
ötlet (10) idea
ötödik (5) fifth
ott (2) there
otthon (3) at home
palacsinta (8) pancake
pálinka (6) brandy like drink
papir (4) paper
paprika (7) bell pepper
papucs (7) slippers
paradicsom (7) tomato
parkol (4) park sg
parkoló (4) parking lot
pedig (1) but
pénz (10) money
pénzváltó (4) money-changer
pezsgő (8) champagne
piac (10) market
pincér (6) waiter
piritós (9) toast
piros (7) red
pizsama kabát (9) pajama top
pohár (8) glass, cup
polc (7) shelf
pontosan (7) exactly
portás (4) front desk clerk
posta (2) post office
próbafülke (7) fitting room
probléma (9) problem
program (10) program
ráismer (6) recognize
rántott hús (8) breaded cutlet
rántott-sajt (6) breaded cheese
ráz (9) shake
reggel (2) morning
reggeli (4) breakfast
reggelizik (4) have breakfast
régóta (6) long (since)
remek (10) magnificent
rend (2) order
rendelés (6) order
rendez (10) organize
repülőgép (1) airplane
repülőtér (1) airport
repülőút (3) flight
részleg (9) division
rétes (8) strudel
rizs (6) rice
rokon (1) relative

rózsaszín **(7)** pink
ruha **(2)** clothes
ruha **(7)** dress
ruházat **(7)** clothing
sajt **(7)** cheese
saláta **(7)** lettuce
sápadt **(9)** pale
sárga **(7)** yellow
sarok **(5)** corner
segít **(7)** help
sem **(3)** neither
sérült **(9)** wounded
séta **(6)** walk
siet **(7)** hurry
sofőr **(3)** driver
sok **(3)** many, much
sonka **(7)** ham
sor **(1)** row
sötétkék **(7)** dark blue
sült-krumpli **(6)** fried potatoes
száj **(9)** mouth
száll **(1)** fly (v)
szállás **(4)** accommodation
szállít **(10)** ship, transport
szálloda **(5)** hotel
szalonna **(7)** bacon
számla **(3)** bill
száraz **(6)** dry
szédül **(9)** be dizzy
szék **(1)** chair
szekrény **(5)** cupboard
szem **(9)** eyes
szemben **(4)** opposite to
személy **(6)** person
szemüveg **(1)** glasses
szép **(2)** nice
szerencse **(1)** luck
szerencsés **(3)** lucky
szeret **(6)** like, love
szerint **(3)** according to
szerződés **(10)** contract
szigorú **(9)** strict
szilva **(7)** plum
színek **(7)** colors
színház **(5)** theatre
szív **(9)** heart
szobapincér **(4)** room service waiter
szoknya **(7)** skirt
szól **(4)** speak, say, talk
szolgálat **(4)** service
szőlő **(7)** grapes
szórakozás **(6)** entertainment,
                     going out
szörnyen **(9)** awfully

szükség **(1)** need
születik **(2)** be born
szülő **(10)** parent
szürke **(7)** grey
talál **(8)** find
találkozik **(3)** meet sy
tanár **(1)** teacher
tárcsáz **(8)** dial
társadalmi élet **(10)** social life
társadalom **(10)** society
tart **(1)** go to
tartózkodik **(2)** stay at
táska **(5)** bag
taxi **(2)** taxi, cab
taxiállomás **(3)** cabstand
te **(2)** you
tea **(9)** tea
tegnap **(9)** yesterday
tej **(7)** milk
telefonszám **(8)** telephone number
térd **(9)** knee
természetesen **(2)** of course
ti **(2)** you (plural)
tizedik **(10)** tenth
több **(1)** more
tojás **(7)** eggs
tökéletes **(7)** perfect
töltött-paprika **(6)** stuffed peppers
töltött káposzta **(8)** stuffed cabbage
trikó **(7)** T-shirt
tud **(3)** know
tüdő **(9)** lungs
túl **(3)** too (much)
tűnik **(9)** appear
turista **(3)** tourist
uborka saláta **(6)** cucumber salad
úgy **(4)** so, that
ugyanaz **(1)** same
újj **(9)** finger
ül **(1)** sit
úr **(6)** Sir, mister
uram **(4)** sir (salutation)
úszómedence **(4)** swimming pool
után **(7)** after
utazik **(1)** travel
utca **(3)** street
útlevél **(2)** passport
üveg **(8)** bottle
üzlet **(1)** business
üzletember **(10)** businessman
vacsora **(3)** dinner
vacsorázik **(4)** have dinner
vagy **(5)** or
vagyok **(1)** (I) am

vagyunk **(1)** (we) are
vaj **(7)** butter
valami **(2)** something
változik **(6)** change
vám **(2)** customs
vámtiszt **(2)** customs officer
vámvizsgálat **(2)** customs examination
vannak **(1)** (they) are
vár **(1)** wait
város **(5)** city, town
vásárlás **(7)** shopping
vásárol **(7)** shop sg
vendégség **(8)** being a guest
vérnyomás **(9)** blood pressure
vese **(9)** kidney
vesz **(3)** take
vesz **(8)** buy
vezet **(6)** drive
vigyáz **(1)** take care of
világoskék **(7)** light blue
villamos **(2)** tram
virág **(8)** flower
visszajön **(7)** return, come back
visszamegy **(1)** return
víz **(10)** water
volt **(3)** was
vonat **(2)** train
vörös **(6)** red
zene **(6)** music
zenekar **(6)** band
zokni **(7)** socks
zöld **(7)** green
zöldség **(7)** vegetable
Zoltán **(1)** <masculine name>
zsemle **(7)** roll

A többi az öné. (3)	Keep the change.
Átnézni valamit. (6)	To take a look at something.
Attól tartok, hogy... (6)	I am afraid that...
Az áruház 6 órakor bezár. (7)	The store closes **at 6** o'clock.
Bocsánat! (1)	Excuse me!
Egészségünkre! (6)	Cheers!
Egy óra múlva. (8)	Within an hour.
Elszokott a magyar konyhától. (9)	He is **not used** to Hungarian food **anymore.**
Engedje meg, hogy bemutatkozzam. (1)	Let me introduce myself.
Fáj a gyomrom. (9)	I have a stomachache.
Fáj a fejem. (9)	I have a headache.
Fáj a torkom. (9)	I have a shore throat.
Hányas a méreted? (7)	What is your size?
Hogy ízlett a vacsora? (6)	How did you like your dinner?
Jó estét kívánok. (6)	Good Evening.
Jó utat! (10)	Have a nice trip.
Jó éjszakát! (8)	Good night!
Jó reggelt! (2)	Good morning!
Kérem szóljanak, ha... (4)	Please ask, if...
Kérem fáradjon a... (2)	Please go to the...
Kérem... (2)	Please...
Komputer programot készít. (10)	He writes computer software.
Köhögök. (9)	I have a cough.
Köszönöm szépen. (2)	Thank you very much.
Köszönöm. (1)	Thank you.
Lázas vagyok. (9)	I have a fever.
Légy szíves! (8)	Please.
Leszedi az asztalt. (8)	She clears the table.
Majd meglátjuk. (8)	We will see.
Meg tudná mondani...? (4)	Can you tell me...?
Meg vagyok fázva. (9)	I have a cold.
Megmérem a lázad. (9)	I take your temperature.
Megrándult a bokám. (9)	I sprained my ankle.
Menjünk haza. (3)	Let's go home.
Mennyi ideig? (2)	For how long?
Mennyibe kerül? (7)	How much does it cost?
Miért ne? (6)	Why not!
Milyen kedves tőlük! (8)	How nice of them!
Nagyon késő van. (8)	It is very late.
Náthás vagyok. (9)	I have the flu.
Nem vagyok benne biztos. (7)	I'm not sure.
Nem tart velem? (6)	Would you care to join me?
Nincs/nincsenek... (1)	There is no/are no...
Örülök hogy megismertem. (10)	Nice to meet you.
Otthon találkozunk. (3)	See you at home.
Parancsoljon. (2)	Here you go.
Rendben van. (3)	It's all right.
Rengeteget ettem. (8)	I ate too much.
Sajnálom. (6)	I am sorry.

Segíthetek? (7)	May I help you?
Sok szerencsét! (10)	Good luck!
Szeretne látni... (1)	She/he would like to see...
Sziasztok! (8)	Hi!
Szívesen. (8)	You are welcome.
Terhes vagyok. (9)	I am pregnant.
Tessék. (3)	Here you go.
Úgy hallottam... (4)	I heard that...
Útbaigazítás kérés. (5)	Asking for directions.
Vigyázzatok magatokra! (10)	Take care of yourselves.
Viszontlátásra! (2)	Good bye!

ENGLISH-HUNGARIAN

Asking for directions. (5)	Útbaigazítás kérés.
Can you tell me...? (4)	Meg tudná mondani...?
Cheers! (6)	Egészségünkre!
Excuse me! (1)	Bocsánat!
For how long? (2)	Mennyi ideig?
Good bye! (2)	Viszontlátásra!
Good evening. (6)	Jó estét kívánok.
Good luck! (10)	Sok szerencsét!
Good morning! (2)	Jó reggelt!
Good night! (8)	Jó éjszakát!
Have a nice trip. (10)	Jó utat!
He is **not used to** Hungarian food **anymore**. (9)	Elszokott a magyar konyhától.
He writes computer software. (10)	Komputer programot készít.
Here you go. (2)	Parancsoljon.
Here you go. (3)	Tessék.
Hi! (8)	Sziasztok!
How did you like your dinner? (6)	Hogy ízlett a vacsora?
How much does it cost? (7)	Mennyibe kerül?
How nice of them! (8)	Milyen kedves tőlük!
I am afraid that... (6)	Attól tartok, hogy...
I am not sure. (7)	Nem vagyok benne biztos.
I am pregnant. (9)	Terhes vagyok.
I am sorry. (6)	Sajnálom.
I ate too much. (8)	Rengeteg ettem.
I have a cold. (9)	Meg vagyok fázva.
I have a cough. (9)	Köhögök.
I have a fever. (9)	Lázas vagyok.
I have a headache. (9)	Fáj a fejem.
I have a shore throat. (9)	Fáj a torkom.
I have a stomachache. (9)	Fáj a gyomrom.
I have the flu. (9)	Náthás vagyok.
I heard that... (4)	Úgy hallottam...
I sprained my ankle. (9)	Megrándult a bokám.
I take your temperature. (9)	Megmérem a lázad.
It's all right. (3)	Rendben van.
It is very late. (8)	Nagyon késő van.
Keep the change. (3)	A többi az öné.
Let me introduce myself. (1)	Engedje meg, hogy bemutatkozzam
Let's go home. (3)	Menjünk haza.
May I help you? (7)	Segíthetek?
Nice to meet you. (10)	Örülök hogy megismertem.
Please ask, if... (4)	Kérem szóljanak, ha...
Please go to the... (2)	Kérem fáradjon a...
Please. (8)	Légy szíves!
Please... (2)	Kérem...
See you at home. (3)	Otthon találkozunk.
She clears the table. (8)	Leszedi az asztalt.
She/he would like to see... (1)	Szeretne látni...
Take care of yourselves. (10)	Vigyázzatok magatokra!
Thank you very much. (2)	Köszönöm szépen.

Thank you. **(1)**	Köszönöm.
The store closes **at 6** o'clock. **(7)**	Az áruház **6** órakor bezár.
There is no/are no... **(1)**	Nincs/nincsenek...
To take a look at something. **(6)**	Átnézni valamit.
We will see. **(8)**	Majd meglátjuk.
What is your size? **(7)**	Hányas a méreted?
Why not! **(6)**	Miért ne?
Within an hour. **(8)**	Egy óra múlva.
Would you care to join me? **(6)**	Nem tart velem?
You are welcome. **(8)**	Szívesen.

A Selection of
Hippocrene

PHRASEBOOKS
AND GRAMMAR AIDS

Arabic Grammar of the Written Language: $19.95 • 0-87052-101-2

Elementary Modern Armenian Grammar: $8.95 • 0-87052-811-4

Czech Phrasebook: $9.95 • 0-87052-967-6

American Phrasebook for Poles: $7.95 • 0-87052-907-2

Polish Phrasebook and Dictionary: $9.95 • 0-7818-0134-6

Romanian Grammar: $6.95 • 0-87052-892-0

Russian Phrasebook and Dictionary: $9.95 • 0-7818-0190-7
Cassettes (separately): $12.95 • 0-7818-0192-3

Spanish Grammar: $8.95 • 0-87052-893-9

Swahili Phrasebook: $6.95 • 0-87052-970-6

Ukrainian Phrasebook and Dictionary: $9.95 • 0-7818-0188-5
Cassettes (separately): $12.95 • 0-7818-0191-5

===============================

TO ORDER FROM HIPPOCRENE, send check or money order for the price of the book plus $4.00 for shipping and handling ($.50 for each additional book) to Hippocrene Books, 171 Madison Avenue, New York, NY 10016.

HIPPOCRENE HANDY
and
EXTRA-HANDY
DICTIONARIES

For the traveler of independent spirit and curious mind, this practical series will help you to communicate, not just to get by. Common phrases are conveniently listed through key words. Pronunciation follows each entry and a reference section reviews all major grammar points.

Handy Extras are extra helpful—offering even more words and phrases for students and travelers.

ARABIC
 $8.95 • 0-87052-960-9
CHINESE
 $6.95 • 0-87052-050-4
CZECH EXTRA
 $8.95 • 0-7818-0138-9
DUTCH
 $6.95 • 0-87052-049-0
FRENCH
 $6.95 • 0-7818-0010-2
GERMAN
 $6.95 • 0-7818-0014-5
GREEK
 $8.95 • 0-87052-961-7
HUNGARIAN EXTRA
 $8.95 • 0-7818-0164-8
ITALIAN
 $6.95 • 0-7818-0011-0

JAPANESE
 $6.95 • 0-87052-962-5
KOREAN
 $8.95 • 0-7818-0082-X
PORTUGUESE
 $6.95 • 0-87052-053-9
RUSSIAN
 $6.95 • 0-7818-0013-7
SERBO-CROATIAN
 $6.95 • 0-87052-051-2
SPANISH
 $6.95 • 0-7818-0012-9
SWEDISH
 $6.95 • 0-87052-054-7
THAI
 $8.95 • 0-87052-963-3
TURKISH
 $6.95 • 0-87052-982-X

Slovakia Cartographia Country Map

Brand new for Fall 1993! • *$4.95* • *ISBN 0-7818-0195-8*

- This comprehensive map includes topography, roads, and landmarks
- Includes inserts of city maps of Bratislava and Kosice
- Covers all of Slovakia plus the surrounding regions
- Convenient index of place names
- Handy and durable
- Other up-to-date maps available: Albania, Baltic States (Estonia, Latvia, Lithuania), Bulgaria, Bratislava City Map, Czech Republic, Bucharest City Map, Hungary Road Map, Warsaw City Map, Prague City Map, Romania, Yugoslavia, Poland, and more!

From the Publisher of:

All Along the Danube by Marina Polvay. The cookbook with recipes covering the countries that border the Danube River....From Germany to Romania, these Eastern European recipes are sure to bring back the taste of the old country. Marina Polvay is an internationally renowned cook and consultant for restaurants worldwide.

_____$11.95 paperback   349 pages   ISBN 0-7818-0098-6

Slovak-English/English-Slovak Dictionary by Nina Trnka. Compact and comprehensive for travelers, businessmen and students of English or Slovak. Contains 7,500 entries with easy-to-follow pronunciation in both sections.

_____$8.95   360 pages   ISBN 0-87052-115-2

=============================

TO ORDER FROM HIPPOCRENE, send for a free catalog, or send a check or money order for the price of the book or map plus $4.00 for shipping and handling to Hippocrne Books, 171 Madison Avenue, New York, NY 10016.